ENDORSEMENTS

Jeanne Damoff beautifully weaves a tale of finding what is lost at the same time as grieving what can never be again . . . and learning to love better in the process. Insightful, haunting, a tale of trial and acceptance, loss and rebirth, and the unexpected graces God gives when He has seemed to take away that which we most held dear, this book is for anybody whose life didn't turn out quite the way they expected.

—Lisa Samson,
Christy Award winning author
of *The Church Ladies, Quaker Summer,*
and *Justice in the Burbs*

Parting the Waters is a book about authentic, gritty struggle during loss. Author Jeanne Damoff paints a vivid picture of her family's journey through her son's drowning accident, ~~but she does so with broad enough~~ strokes that the reader gleans comfo   nal tragedy. If you are suffering from g   ns, or anger, *Parting the Waters* is a muc

                                        ...uth,
author of *Ordinary Mom, Extraordinary God*
(Harvest House, 2005) and
Pioneer Parenting (WaterBrook, 2006)

Parting the Waters demonstrates the way in which divine grace and human prayer can alter what we expect the course of events to be, such that those two mighty forces in modern American life, namely medicine and law, are, to their own great surprise and joy, thoroughly disrupted and outflanked. And thereby redeemed. The pictures Jeanne Damoff draws of doctors and judges being confounded by turns of events—and being *glad* of being confounded—are heartbreakingly beautiful. And the combination of fearless honesty, deep Christian faith, and utter matter-of-factness in her way of telling the story make the book a great read. It is my pleasure to give *Parting the Waters* my strongest endorsement.

—Dr. Rick Steele,
author and professor of theology,
Seattle Pacific University

Parting the Waters offers healing and spiritual insight even to those of us who have not been cut so deeply. In so many ways our financial struggles are worlds apart from what the Damoff family had to deal with, and yet it is still amazing how many of the same spiritual battles must be fought. Anger, depression, guilt, self-pity. . . . And also that terrible humbling when so many people reach out and care for you in ways that you will never be able to repay.

Readers will take away practical advice as well as get a dose of spiritual meat. Small things, like Jeanne's praying blessings for the families and individuals that sacrificed for her family. I think there will be folks who will read that and say, "Wow, there is something I can *do* to repay these people." It is an important step away from being focused inward.

You would not believe how many times in the past couple of months I would have given this book away if I had a hard copy. When it gets published I want to order at least half a dozen so I can keep a stash handy, ready to give away.

—Megan Yerkes,
homeschooling mother of six

As I read this book, I came to understand even better that if I were to continue to become the man I desire to be, more suffering would bring it about—more sorrows, and more trials. God has given me the faith at this point to know in my heart and act as if He can be trusted. Jesus was the Man of Sorrows, well acquainted with suffering and aloneness. I want to be like Him.

Sure enough, shortly after I finished reading *Parting the Waters,* I ran into a firestorm of my sixteen-year-old son's rebellion and acting out (underage drinking, etc.). After reading this book, I was able to actively enter into that situation with faith and trust that it would work out for good.

—Craig Smitham,
attorney

Parting the Waters was wonderful! Jeanne did a great job blending the story, the medical facts and the emotional processes that she endured. It brought a lot of 'life' and encouragement to me, as I'm confident it brings to all who read it. It really causes the heavenly view to come more into focus. How we desperately need to gain more of an eternal perspective.

—Karla Anders,
cancer survivor

I first met Jacob when Natalie, his best friend, shared the story of their friendship in *Real Teens, Real Stories, Real Life.* This is more than a story of a near-drowning experience. It is a beautiful example of faith, love, perseverance, and hope in the face of tragedy.

—T. Suzanne Eller,
author, speaker, and founder of
Real Teen Faith

PARTING
THE
WATERS

A TRUE STORY

PARTING
THE
WATERS

FINDING BEAUTY *in* BROKENNESS

JEANNE DAMOFF

WINEPRESS WP PUBLISHING

WinePress Publishing (PO Box 428, Enumclaw, WA 98022) functions only as book publisher. As such, the ultimate design, content, editorial accuracy, and views expressed or implied in this work are those of the author.

ISBN 13: 978-1-57921-950-5
ISBN 10: 1-57921-950-0
Library of Congress Catalog Card Number: 2008921218

For Jacob

He sank from sight, but not unseen—
Omnipotence chose not to intervene.
"Beyond the brokenness
The beauty lies.

Open your eyes."

Until a pebble falls,
The calm remains;
But in the ripples lie
Life's greatest gains.

CONTENTS

ACKNOWLEDGMENTS

In many ways, the real heroes of this story are the people, businesses, and churches that rallied around our family as the tale told on the following pages unfolded. Some will be mentioned by name. Many will not. In fact, I don't even know who they all are. As inadequate as it may be, I offer my heartfelt gratitude to everyone who reached out to Jacob and our family in countless ways. You know who you are, and—more importantly—God does, too. I pray your reward in heaven will be magnificent.

Any type of writing can feel a little like bleeding on the page, but telling a deeply personal story requires a frightening degree of vulnerability. The following writers and publishing industry professionals offered priceless advice and encouragement as this story took shape. Critique partners: Vickie Phelps, Pamela Dowd, Nanci Huyser, and Ruth Gillette. Authors: Mary DeMuth, Lisa Samson, T. Suzanne Eller, Cecil Murphey, Deidre Knight, Deborah Gyapong, Susan Meissner, and Madison Richards. Editors: Bonnie Perry, Mick Silva, Mary McNeil, Vicki Crumpton, Denny and Philis Boultinghouse, David Kopp, Tony Collins, Kim Bangs, and Andy Meissenheimer. The folks at WinePress Publishing: Athena Dean, Carla Williams, George Dillaway, and Adam Cothes. And my wise, wonderful, and supportive literary agent, Wendy Lawton of Books & Such Literary Agency.

Special thanks to the many family members and dear friends who prayed for me as I wrote, read early drafts and offered great feedback, and who remain a part of our ongoing journey. They include my parents, Jim and Patsy Leftwich; siblings, Lois Leftwich, Sharon Miller, and Jim Leftwich; family members, Sharon Damoff, Jeanne McAlpin, Patsy Keller, Nathan Miller, and Anna Miller Sanders; and friends, Jeff Franzen, Craig Smitham, Karla Anders, Megan Yerkes, Jill Hale, Jennifer Dodson, Kathy Kurtz, Terri Frazier, Becky Cline, Ileaine Cline, and Natalie Dowd Grubbs.

Extra special thanks to my beloved traveling companions, George, Jacob, Grace, Luke, and Curtis. You are my heart.

And most special thanks to God, who took our brokenness and created unbelievable beauty. May the ripples continue.

AUTHOR'S NOTE

This is a true story. However, when we found ourselves swept along by these events, for some reason (silly me!) I didn't have the foresight to carry a tape recorder in my pocket. As a result, when the time came to write the story, I couldn't reconstruct every conversation word for word. Nor could I recreate every scene to perfection in all its particulars. Was his shirt blue or green? Did we drink coffee or tea? (Does it matter?)

And yet I wanted to tell a story, not preach a sermon, or formulate Seven Easy Steps for Successful Suffering.

So, you're getting a story. And my promise to the reader is that, in every instance, essential truth has been communicated. All the people are real. All the events unfolded as told. No kindness has been exaggerated. No heroic deed overdrawn.

God took a broken boy and set ripples in motion that spread through an entire community and beyond. On these pages I've attempted to honestly share our battles against fear, self-pity, anger, and confusion as well as our glimpses into God's good and glorious purposes. Accomplishing those goals mattered more to me than whether someone said "Hi" or "Hello." I hope the reader will feel the same way.

I'm honored you've chosen to read our story. If our journey encourages you in your own struggles, I'd love to hear from you. You can find my contact information on my web site, www.jeannedamoff.com.

You'll also find a photo album containing shots of people you'll meet in this book. Please do stop by!

Jeanne Damoff
February, 2008

PROLOGUE

Yet you do not know what your life will be like tomorrow.

—Jas. 4:14

Late in the afternoon on Wednesday, May 22, 1996, the phone rang. I dropped my laundry basket in the utility room and darted through the kitchen to snatch the receiver before the answering machine picked up the call.

"Hi, Mom!" Jacob sounded excited.

"Jacob. Where are you?"

"I'm at Kevin's. He wants me to spend the night tonight and go to the eighth-grade canoeing party tomorrow."

As a ninth grader, Jacob had just completed his final exams. Thursday was a free day for freshmen. Kevin's teacher had approved the boys' plans, so I didn't see any reason why he shouldn't go. Jacob asked if I'd bring him some clothes and a toothbrush.

"Sure. Do you need a swimsuit? Or money?"

"We're not swimming, but I do need money." He laughed. "A couple hundred dollars should be enough."

"Right. Very cute. Anything in particular you want to wear?"

"Um . . . yeah. Bring that purple cow shirt Adam gave me, and my black shorts."

"OK. I'll be over in about ten minutes."

I replaced the cordless phone in its base and headed up the stairs to Jacob's room. Even though I knew what to expect, the utter chaos stopped me at the door. What a slob. I sighed, but—affection conquering disgust—I waded in. The black shorts lay in the middle of the floor. Now to find the cow T-shirt.

I kicked aside his maroon corduroys and the "new" blue-and-white plaid, double-knit slacks he'd bought at Good Will for fifty cents. Jacob loved those tacky pants. Their appeal eluded me, but I couldn't help feeling proud of his trend-setter ways. He managed to gain approval from his peers, no matter what he wore.

After almost tripping on his skateboard, I scooted it behind the electric guitar stand and lifted a photograph from the floor. Jacob and his best friend, Natalie, on a roller coaster at Six Flags—him with unruly, blond curls and mischievous, blue eyes; her with beautiful fair skin and flaming red hair. Both of them laughing. I smiled at their youthful enthusiasm, then chuckled to myself. I felt like the one on a roller coaster.

Watching my oldest child blossom into early adulthood had been a wild-but-fun adventure. He was smart, funny, talented, and interesting. I liked who he was becoming. Who wants boring children? I pushed aside his comforter, which lay in a crumpled heap on the floor. Ah! The purple cow shirt.

I stuffed the items in a small duffel bag, grabbed my purse off the kitchen counter, and stepped outside into what felt like a sauna. Heat shimmered off the hood of our navy-blue Suburban. My energy level wilted as I thought ahead to the next few months. Summer always overstayed her welcome in East Texas.

Sweat dripped down my legs. My shorts stuck to me as I slid into the SUV, which I could have sworn had been preheated to 400 degrees. I turned the key, punched the AC button, and pushed the fan speed to max.

Five minutes later I drove past Trinity Episcopal School, where my three children attended and I taught Bible to all the grades from pre-school to junior high. I glanced at the empty building. Only one more day of school, then summer vacation. I needed a break as much as the kids did.

Kevin's parents owned a large, historic home a few blocks from Trinity. I loved the restored older homes in that neighborhood. As I turned onto their street, I amused myself by imagining the ancient hardwood trees wore broad, leafy hats to provide shade from the sun's relentless rays. Pulling into Kevin's driveway, I hopped out of the SUV, scooped up the duffel bag, and knocked on the screen door. I leaned close and peered into the unlit kitchen.

Entering the room from a hallway, a shirtless, smiling Jacob emerged from the shadows. It seemed like almost overnight he'd lost his soft, little boy look. His physique was becoming more and more like his father's—lean and muscular.

Jacob opened the screen and took the bag. Without a word he released the door and sauntered away.

You're welcome. Nice to see you, too, Jacob.

Knowing Jacob, he was probably in the middle of an "important" video game. I called after him the words I often say when parting with my children: "I love you. Be careful."

He paused and looked back over his shoulder. "I love you, too. I will." Then he disappeared into the dark hallway.

I'm not sure what I would have done if I'd known what lay ahead. But I wouldn't have just driven away.

Not if I'd known this would be my last conversation with Jacob for a long time.

CHAPTER 1

A PEBBLE FALLS

But now, thus says the LORD, your Creator, O Jacob, and He who formed you, O Israel, "Do not fear, for I have redeemed you; I have called you by name; you are Mine! When you pass through the waters, I will be with you; and through the rivers, they will not overflow you."

—Isa. 43:1–2

I eased our aging Suburban into a tight space in front of Trinity's upper-school campus—a rented, gray-brick, office building two blocks away from the elementary school. I'd just returned from chaperoning the seventh-grade class party at Putt-Putt Golf and Games in Longview, thirty miles away. My daughter, Grace, and her classmates piled out of the SUV, laughing and shoving each other. As I watched their antics over my shoulder, I checked off one more duty on my mental list. I could almost taste summer.

Glancing at the school entrance, I noticed a fellow teacher, Pam Cheatham, crying. I reached for the door handle, then startled at seeing Pam's husband, Brent, right outside my window.

He opened the door and grasped my arm as I slid out of the seat. "There's been an accident. You need to come with us." Still gripping my arm, Brent led me toward his van.

My mind rebelled against the ominous words. "What? An accident?"

I scanned the grassy schoolyard. Students and teachers stood alone or in clumps with stunned expressions—like lost sheep. Confusion clouded my mind. I turned to Brent. "What's going on? What happened?"

He didn't look at me. His mouth was set in a grim line. "We'll tell you on the way to the hospital." His firm clasp on my elbow propelled me forward. We'd almost reached his van.

The hospital! What about my children?

I yanked my arm away from Brent and spun around, searching for Grace's petite frame and long, blonde hair among the students. Her widened eyes met mine across the lawn, alarm dawning in her expression. She looked frozen, her face pale.

I wanted to go to her, but . . . Something was terribly wrong. My eyes skimmed the yard again, but I couldn't spot my fifth-grade son, Luke. School was out. I couldn't just leave them.

Pam met Brent and me at their minivan and opened the back door. They practically pushed me inside.

I hesitated, one foot still on the ground. "What about Grace and Luke?"

"Don't worry; someone will bring them," Brent said. He hurried around to the driver's seat.

This is insane! I slid the back door shut, and Brent pulled away from the curb. I kept my eyes on Grace until I heard Pam erupt into uncontrolled crying.

She choked out her words. "There was . . . some kind of accident at the lake. . . . I don't know if it involved the canoes. . . ."

An accident at the lake? Jacob!

"Jeremy Maxey is dead!" Sobs convulsed her. "He drowned!"

"What?" I strained forward against the seat belt, trying to get closer to the front seat. "Are you sure? Was anyone else hurt?" With all my heart I hoped they needed me as a Bible teacher.

"Jacob is in the hospital. . . ."

Oh, Lord, please, no!

Pam took a deep breath, trying to regain control. "I don't know what his condition is. George is waiting for you there."

I prayed out loud. For help, for mercy, for wisdom, for Jeremy's family. For Jacob. I prayed in circles until I didn't know what else to pray.

Then we rode in silence. A cloak of composure concealed a mind that darted from fear to fear, finally pausing on the only comforting news I'd heard so far.

George was at the hospital.

A few hours earlier my husband had been working in his office at East Texas Baptist University when the phone rang in the office next door. He heard the biology department chairman answer. Moments later, Roy Darville leaned out his door and said, "Hey, George, you have a call. You can take it on my phone."

George stepped into Roy's office and picked up the receiver. "This is George Damoff."

Elizabeth, the secretary at Trinity Episcopal Church, sounded shaken. "Father Jones just called from Caddo Lake. Something serious has happened to Jacob, and he said I should call and let you know he'd be getting in touch with you."

"Something serious?" George suppressed the sense of dread that swept over him. "What do you mean? Is Jacob OK?"

"I'm sorry. I don't have any details, but he should be calling soon . . ."

The phone in George's office rang. "I'm getting another call," George interrupted. "Maybe it's him. Thank you." He bolted into his office and grabbed the receiver.

Philip Jones, Trinity Episcopal Church's rector and a chaperone at the canoeing party, was calling from a restaurant pay phone. He seemed to be gasping for air, and his voice cracked. "George, I'm so sorry. . . . I was too late. . . . we tried everything—CPR for twenty minutes . . ."

"What? Philip, I can't understand you!" George struggled to make sense of the emotional, disjointed message. As the truth sank in, a hideous claw squeezed his heart. Philip was groping for words to break the news of Jacob's death.

At the same moment, someone ran toward Philip shouting that Jacob had begun to breathe. Philip's anguish exploded into hysterical weeping and shouts of relief. "Jacob is alive! Oh, thank You, God! Jacob is breathing!"

Frustrated, George knew he wouldn't get much more information from Philip. Then he heard an ambulance siren in the background. "I'm going to the hospital." He hung up.

Ten minutes later George entered the ER and approached a nurse. "My son was in an accident at Caddo Lake. He's on his way here."

"Yes, sir. We received a call."

"Would you please notify Dr. Orin Littlejohn?"

George knew the ambulance drive from Caddo Lake back to Marshall would take about half an hour. He positioned himself at the emergency room entrance. As the minute hand inched its way around the clock, he stood trancelike in the sunlight streaming through the window, refusing to let any clear thought possess his mind. He would wait until he could assess the situation himself.

Dr. Littlejohn, our family physician, arrived from his office across the street and greeted George. Though Dr. Littlejohn tried to engage him in conversation, George kept his eyes fixed on the driveway outside. His mind was occupied in a battle against panic.

Finally the ambulance pulled in front of the door. As soon as Jacob's feet emerged, fear seized George's heart. He watched the paramedics wheel in Jacob's shivering, unconscious body on a gurney. Jacob's face was pale, his breathing shallow and irregular.

George followed them into an ER examining room where a team of medical personnel hustled into action. The cartoonish cow face on Jacob's favorite T-shirt mocked the severity of the scene. As though declaring the days of levity gone forever, skilled hands cut through the damp clothing to remove it. A respiratory therapist sat beside Jacob's head and used a hand pump to force air into his lungs. Nurses prepared to insert IVs. "We love you, Jacob," George shouted as attendants ushered him from the room.

By the time Brent parked his van at the ER entrance to let me out, Jacob had been admitted and moved to ICU. George appeared at the door before I landed both feet on the pavement.

Relief flooded over me when I saw him. I didn't want to face this alone. When I reached George he took both my hands in his.

A hundred questions crowded my brain, but one urgent thought pressed to the front: "We need to pray."

"Yes. We need to pray." His voice sounded gruff.

I wanted George to tell me everything was going to be OK. Hoping for a good sign, I scanned the face I'd known and loved for seventeen years. His firm jaw, the rugged features that complemented his love of the outdoors, those striking blue eyes—they looked back at me now with a steadiness I'd learned to depend on. But fear lurked there, too, refusing to cooperate with his banishment orders.

Familiar faces filled the waiting area, teenagers hugging, people crying in small huddles. I didn't want to talk to any of them. I wanted assurance from George. "How is Jacob?"

"He's . . . I'm not sure. . . . Jeanne, he's very sick. Come on." He turned and indicated a nurse standing behind him. "We're supposed to go somewhere and talk with Philip. This nurse is taking us."

The nurse led us down a long hall. We passed a room with curtains drawn across the glass wall. George leaned toward me and whispered, "Jeremy's family is in there."

I hadn't been thinking about Jeremy. The horror of it all crashed over me. I tried to walk, but my legs didn't want to obey my brain.

"I think I might faint."

George supported me as the nurse led us into an empty examining room. We sat in dazed silence and waited for Philip to join us there.

Unknown to us, Philip had arrived from the lake soaked and distraught. Ten or more local pastors from various denominations had already gathered in the ER waiting area. When Philip staggered into the room, they encircled him, united as one in prayer for their fellow shepherd.

Bolstered by their support, Philip joined us in the examining room. A tall man with coal-black hair, he had exchanged his priest's collar that day for a maroon polo shirt and jeans—vestments for a pleasant spring outing with his daughter's class. Now, damp from head to foot, he perched on the edge of the bed. We sat in chairs opposite him, waiting. I dreaded hearing what I longed to know.

As Philip began to speak, I listened as one in a twilight zone, hearing the recitation of facts, but unable to connect my emotions. Philip explained that the students and adults had divided into small groups to ride in canoes. At least six adult chaperones were present, including two Texas state game wardens. The group enjoyed paddling canoes all morning and stopped near a marina at noon to eat. After lunch, some of the kids splashed and waded in the water near the boat ramp. Swimming hadn't been on the agenda, but it was a hot day.

When the time came to load the canoes and continue, Jacob and Jeremy were missing. Someone checked the bathrooms at the nearby restaurant. No sign of the boys. Students and chaperones fanned out, calling their names.

On an impulse, Philip pulled off his shirt and shoes and dove into the murky water to search, swimming along the bottom, hands groping in the darkness. He had no idea where to look, and it was impossible to see anything below the surface.

After several dives, Philip felt a body on the lake bottom at a place where the water is about fourteen feet deep. He grabbed, pulling Jacob to the surface, unconscious and blue. He yelled, "I've got Jacob!"

The kids on shore went berserk when they realized what was happening. As soon as Philip got Jacob on land, some of the adults started CPR. Philip and several others dove to search for Jeremy. The remaining chaperones tried to calm the kids.

Sandra McPhail, a woman in the restaurant, came out and coordinated the CPR efforts. They tried for almost twenty minutes. No response.

At that point, Philip had located a phone and called George.

Philip spoke to us with feeling and dramatic gestures, but I felt distant and unattached, like a woman hearing someone else's tragic story.

He couldn't be talking about Jacob. This couldn't be happening. But it was.

Jerking myself back to the present, I remembered Philip had come straight from the lake to the hospital and must be exhausted. "You're still in your wet clothes."

He looked down as if noticing his soggy condition for the first time. "Yeah," he agreed with a sad laugh, "I guess I should go get cleaned up." He looked at George and then me, his eyes bearing the sympathy of a priest and parent. "I'll be back."

"Thanks for all you've done." George's voice was hoarse with quiet emotion. "You're our hero."

After Philip left the room, we sat in numb silence, staring at the wet spot he'd left on the bed. Reality pressed in around us, cold and threatening. By a conservative estimate, at least ten minutes had elapsed while Jacob was underwater, and it had taken another twenty to revive him. We joined hands and prayed for our son.

George and I had begun praying for our children before they were born. We trusted God's promises and believed He had created them for His own purposes. His love for Jacob far surpassed ours. Faith joined fear in my heart as we committed Jacob to the Lord's care once again. But fear remained.

We rode the elevator to the third floor. Apprehension escorted me down the hall toward ICU. A sign on the door limited visitors to one at a time. George waited outside as a nurse led me into the patient area. She reached for the curtain. I took a deep breath.

CHAPTER 2

FIRST RIPPLES

Hold us quiet through the age-long minute
While Thou art silent, and the wind is shrill:
Can the boat sink while Thou, dear Lord, art in it?
Can the heart faint that waiteth on Thy will?

—Amy Carmichael

Tubes, wires, and monitors crowded the space around the bed, engulfing Jacob in an antiseptic jungle. With machine-pumped oxygen bringing a healthy-looking blush to his cheeks, the scene brought both relief and sorrow. I reached for his tousled, curly hair.

"We haven't had a chance to wash his hair yet," the nurse apologized.

Wrapping a strand around my finger, I looked at the sandy grit on his scalp.

Jacob. I'm so sorry.

When Jacob was thirteen months old, I spent a weekend at Children's Hospital in Houston. A friend's four-year-old daughter had contracted a rare virus that attacks the central nervous system, causing serious brain damage or death.

The people who camped in that waiting room lived with constant fear and sorrow.

Several times a day nurses evacuated visitors from the ICU patient area, signifying a little soldier had lost the battle.

Heart-breaking images replayed in my head as I drove the long road from Houston to our former home in Nacogdoches. Like a junkie desperate for a fix, I burst into the kitchen, swept my chubby toddler into my arms, and headed for the backyard. Intercepting George's inquisitive glance, I blurted, "I just need some time with a healthy child."

Large hardwood trees formed a canopy over our heads, and the grass was a cool carpet under my bare feet. Jacob and I were worlds away from glaring lights, white uniforms, broken bodies, and wounded souls. Meandering through the yard, we stopped often to examine an interesting twig or to sniff honeysuckle and taste its nectar.

I pressed my cheek against Jacob's blond curls, holding him as close as I could without crushing him. He giggled, unaware of the fear that gripped my heart. With the vision of dying children fresh in my mind, I longed to shield him. Like the thick branches standing sentinel against the sun, I wanted to stand as a barrier between Jacob and all that is painful and destructive in the world. "God, You know I wouldn't be able to handle seeing Jacob suffer. Please protect my precious baby." I knew only the Lord could keep him safe and well in the days and years to come. I couldn't do it.

And I didn't.

The nurse escorted me back to the waiting room, where I spotted George conferring with Dr. Littlejohn. I joined them, standing close to George.

Dr. Littlejohn explained, "Jacob is receiving 'paralyzing' drugs to keep him asleep. His body needs time to recover from the trauma he's been through before we discontinue the drugs and let him wake up."

"Will he wake up as soon as you stop the drugs?" I wanted assurance.

"That's what we hope will happen," he replied in his kind, fatherly manner. "Meanwhile, the hospital will conduct blood tests, x-rays, and scans to determine Jacob's condition. The contaminated water introduced into his respiratory system could cause pneumonia or other infections. The tests will help us know what we're dealing with, and then we'll take it from there."

"What about brain damage?" George asked.

I winced.

Dr. Littlejohn paused. "We'll just have to wait and see. Until Jacob wakes up, there's no way to know what damage, if any, was done to his brain. Meanwhile, we can pray and hope for the best."

Wait and see. But how long would we have to wait? And what would we see? I couldn't endure the thought of brain damage. Jacob had to get well.

While several people had been attempting to revive Jacob on the shore, a few men had continued diving to search for Jeremy. They located his body after thirty minutes. Though concern for Jacob consumed me, I also felt the impact of Jeremy's death. It was all so unbelievable. Questions abounded, but answers were in short supply.

Jacob was a strong swimmer. How could he drown with all those people around?

In the aftermath, Jeremy's aunt said he couldn't swim. Did Jacob try to help Jeremy and go down with him? I doubted it. Jacob had taken Red Cross Life Saving and knew better than to attempt a solo rescue. He would have called for help.

Did Jeremy start to sink, panic, and grab for whatever he could find, the nearest object being Jacob? How could such a struggle remain un-noticed with all those responsible adults present?

No one saw or heard anything. One of the game wardens mentioned his discomfort when the students started playing in the water. But he didn't see the boys go under. No one saw. It wouldn't have taken much. Just one kid . . . just one adult . . . a cry for help . . .

Why did they let those kids get in the water? And why did Jeremy try to swim if he knew he couldn't?

These were only the first questions. Many more followed. Meanwhile, Jacob lay unconscious in ICU, breathing with the help of a respirator, connected to monitors, tubes, and IVs. And no amount of questioning would change reality.

⎯⎯◆❈◆⎯⎯

Grace and Luke arrived at the hospital with friends. Relief surged through me when I saw my other children for the first time since being whisked away from the school. But I also felt anxious. How were they handling this?

George and I gathered them into a group hug. After a few moments I said, "Grace, you can go in and see Jacob if you want to."

She pulled away. "No." Her voice was quiet but determined. "I don't want to see him." She turned her back on us and headed straight into the waiting area.

The warning in her eyes told me she'd already built a wall around her pain and wasn't ready to let anyone in yet. I decided to give her some space. What had Grace and Luke been hearing and thinking all afternoon? How would we help them through this?

When a young nurse offered to take eleven-year-old Luke into ICU, he followed without hesitation. I tagged along, unsure what his reaction would be. The nurse drew back the curtain, and Luke's eyes opened wide as he looked first at Jacob and then at the hospital apparatus. With his wire-rimmed glasses and straight brown hair, Luke resembled a spellbound Harry Potter.

The nurse watched him and, after a few moments, spoke in a soft tone. "What do you think of all this?"

Luke paused. "Expensive."

Caught off guard, the nurse laughed. I smiled but wasn't surprised. An optimist in general, Luke greeted all of life with expectant curiosity. He would most likely communicate whatever was on his mind. Grace, on the other hand, had always been a reserved child. She might look like a fairy-tale princess, but there was nothing dainty about her resolve. If she chose to conceal her feelings, no one would be able to pry them out of her.

I imagined Luke would be OK. Grace caused me more concern.

⁕

Hoping to hear an encouraging report, Jacob's friends, their parents, church members, school personnel, and others from the community filled the ICU waiting room and the adjacent hallways. One visitor counted three hundred people. Hospital staff, marveling at the multitude, brought out carts filled with snacks and drinks.

Day wore on into night, but the crowds didn't thin much. We all stood watching the news on the waiting-room TV, as the anchorwoman reported the afternoon's tragic events. Jacob had already been taken away by ambulance when film crews arrived, but video footage captured the anguish over Jeremy's death. An exhausted diver wept on the pier after efforts to rescue Jeremy failed.

The report ended with a comment about Jacob's current condition and hospitalization. Everyone in the room looked at George and me.

Somebody, say something! I shook off my surreal nightmare to break the awkward silence. "Well, I sure am glad we have news reporters to let us know how Jacob Duh-MOFF is doing." I mocked the mispronunciation of our last name. No one wants to say DAM-off.

People smiled and seemed to relax. A few chuckled. I returned their smiles, as if to say, "Please be satisfied. We are handling everything just fine."

Muffled conversations sprouted around me. The chatter faded into the background, and I stared at the now-blank TV screen as a scene replayed in my mind. Face buried in his hands, a grief-stricken diver wept beside a lake that had stolen my son.

⁕

A little later, Dr. Littlejohn approached George and me. "You should probably go on home and try to get some rest." He paused. "And I think it would be good if you called your families."

I didn't want to alarm our families. Why scare everyone? Jacob might wake up soon and be fine. "Maybe we should wait a few days and call them when we have more definite information."

He mustered a sad smile. "I think it would be best if you go ahead and call them now."

Marshall Regional Hospital's entrance was just a short block from our front door. I appreciated the convenience but wished with all my heart we didn't need it. We stepped out of the hospital's cold brightness into the muggy warmth of an East Texas night. George and I didn't talk much as we trudged home under a starry sky to make some very difficult telephone calls.

CHAPTER 3

BREAKERS

Why are you in despair, O my soul? And why have you become disturbed within me? . . . All Your breakers and Your waves have rolled over me.

—Ps. 42:5, 7

I sat at the desk in our bedroom. George brought the cordless phone from the hallway and sat nearby on the edge of the bed. To my own amazement I hadn't shed a single tear, and I still didn't cry as we shared the news with one family member after another.

When we called my sister Sharon, however, she dissolved into quiet sobs almost as soon as we uttered our first sentence. She wasn't hysterical. She was broken with sorrow. I knew she would faithfully pray.

Other family members, though sobered by the news, tried to remain upbeat and positive. Some made immediate plans to come to Marshall. We promised to keep everyone informed.

After the phone calls, George and I sat alone in a big, silent house. Weary and numb, we discussed strategy for the immediate future. Grace and Luke had gone to spend the night with friends, but we needed to organize routines for the days ahead. We had no idea how long Jacob would be in the hospital. Regular plans and activities would have to be put on hold or managed in new ways. Fortunately, we had all summer to concentrate on Jacob's getting well. Our calendar was, for the most part, empty.

I saw God's mercy in the timing, and the thought upset me. Why did God time this at all? Even in these earliest hours of uninvited, undesired affliction, I feared for the potential damage to our faith and begged God to preserve it. We didn't understand His plan, but we knew we couldn't endure this hell without Him.

When George and I awoke the next morning, we forced ourselves to gobble a quick breakfast and returned to the hospital. All that day we lived from minute to minute, watching Jacob's monitors, waiting for test results, hoping for any sign of improvement. Our emotions remained on edge, soaring or plunging with each new report or prediction. Like a dancer changing partners after every song, we spun from despair to elation and back again.

Visitors came and went. Many remained for hours in the waiting room. We felt their support and love. We also felt everyone's sense of helplessness.

My sister Sharon arrived. She offered to take Grace and Luke for an extended visit with their cousins when she returned to Nacogdoches, eighty miles south of Marshall.

We accepted with gratitude, relieved to know they'd be exchanging the ICU waiting room for a backyard swimming pool and constant companionship. Grace and Luke would be in good hands, enabling George and me to concentrate on Jacob.

The second day, the ICU staff moved Jacob into their largest room—a private, glassed-in area—and they allowed several people at a time to visit him. We appreciated the patient way they accommodated us, and we made every effort to respect other patients and their families.

Our days settled into a mind-numbing routine. Wake up early. Walk to the hospital. Stay all day. Try to eat. Walk home late at night. Try to sleep. Repeat the cycle. We thought of little beyond Jacob's condition. Everything in life entered a holding pattern.

Waiting with hope. Waiting with fear. Waiting in slow motion.

Events unfolded in a fog. We'd entered unfamiliar territory and had no choice but to go with the flow. Medical decisions confronted us daily. When choking concerns prompted Jacob's doctors to perform a tracheotomy, we listened to their reasoning and consented to the procedure.

Inside I resisted what seemed like a drastic step, an indication that Jacob's condition was more critical than I wanted to admit. As long as he looked normal, I could tell myself it was only a matter of time until he would be himself again.

The trach contradicted this hope, but I struggled to maintain a positive outlook. If a scar on his throat remained as the only permanent reminder of this ordeal, that wouldn't be too high a price to pay. I sought comfort in that thought as the nurses prepared Jacob for surgery.

Several days after Jacob entered ICU, doctors discontinued the sleep-inducing drugs. They hoped he would awaken, respond to touch or sound, and enable them to assess his chances for recovery. We waited in anticipation. Hours passed. Then a whole day. How long did it take for the drugs to wear off?

For the first time, someone mentioned "coma." I recoiled, as though a fiery branding iron had seared the four hateful letters on my heart. I'd banished that word as far from my thoughts as possible, but now it burned on my consciousness with a white-hot intensity. I could handle "unconscious." That sounded more like sleeping. But coma? No. I couldn't handle coma. God had spared Jacob's life. Jacob had to wake up.

Lord, what are You doing? Can this get any worse?

In the middle of the first week, the seizures began. Excruciating and hideous to watch, they lasted for what seemed an eternity. Jacob's whole body writhed. Every muscle tensed. His face contorted. Spasms twisted his back and extremities into unnatural positions. During these seizures, he clenched down with so much pressure on the hard plastic tube in his mouth that his teeth shifted.

We stood by in anguish and horror, wishing we could do something, praying for an end to his torment. Finally, his body relaxed again and sagged into exhausted unconsciousness. Each time this happened, we were forced to acknowledge the probability that Jacob's brain endured further damage. His doctors added anti-seizure medication to his treatment.

Hollywood's portrayal of coma is far from realistic. Once the paralyzing drugs wore off, Jacob's muscles twitched and flexed in almost constant involuntary movement. Sometimes he opened his eyes in a narrow slit, and we leaned in close, thinking perhaps he could see. At first, waves of hope rolled over us, but as time passed, we realized Jacob was far away in a place where he couldn't reach us.

Choosing to believe we could still reach him, we sang to him, prayed out loud, talked to him, and held his hand. One day George and I joined hands across Jacob's bed. Nurses and visitors bustled around us. Monitors beeped and flashed. We shut them all out, closed our eyes and sang, "In moments like these, I sing out a song, I sing out a love song to Jesus. In moments like these, I lift up my voice, I lift up my voice to the Lord. Singing, 'I love you, Lord . . .'"

George wept as we sang, drinking in the words and drawing strength from them. It was a declaration of faith in a good God, no matter what our hearts or eyes told us. A sacrifice of praise.

Days had passed since the near drowning, but I still hadn't cried. A small chapel near the ICU provided a quiet sanctuary for families. One evening I went there alone, knelt before the altar, buried my face in my hands, and bared my heart before the Lord. In this private place, I didn't have to be strong.

As I turned my pain toward heaven, tears flowed. Sobs shook me as I huddled on the floor, not knowing what to say, not needing to say anything, just hurting with an unbearable hurt in the presence of God.

Though I taught at the Episcopal school, we attended Evangelical Presbyterian Church. Our pastor, Kirk Werner, and his wife slipped into the chapel. Kirk and Sue knelt on either side of me, placing their hands on my back, saying nothing—just being there with me in silent intercession, helping bear my pain.

Sue was Jacob's youth minister, a vibrant, godly woman who had led the young people in our church to greater depths of faith and discipleship. I knew she loved Jacob. I knew they both loved our family. But it seemed that no amount of love from any person, or from God Himself, could ever heal the gaping wound in my heart.

"What are we going to do?" The question erupted from my utter helplessness. But I didn't expect an answer. When no more tears would come, I rose from the floor with weary resolve, and went back out to face my shattered son.

I had been through trials before, but I'd never known grief this deep. My heart was a lump of raw pain, so wounded it hurt to breathe. I lay in bed at night wondering if happiness would ever return. I missed the laughter that had filled our lives, the delight and peace that had characterized our home. Would I ever enjoy a whole-body laugh again, the kind that makes your stomach hurt and leaves you gasping for breath, wiping the tears from your eyes?

Our hearts seemed bruised almost beyond healing. George and I bore the same sorrow, yet seldom discussed our pain. We worked together and clung to each other, determined to preserve our faith and family. But a gulf developed between us and widened when I looked into his anguished eyes. George was my best friend, but I couldn't dump my agony on him. Adding my burden to his would be cruel, like asking an exhausted hiker to carry my 150-pound pack as well as his own.

And yet, I also knew I couldn't handle it alone. Who could I trust with the shattered pieces of my heart? I turned to friends, hoping I wouldn't test their friendship beyond the breaking point. Among the many who offered comfort and support, one woman in particular, Pam Dowd, became the embodiment of "a friend in need."

We had moved from Lynchburg, Virginia, to Marshall, Texas, arriving the last week in July, 1992. House hunting topped our agenda, so the first week in August, George and I scheduled an appointment to look at a historic home he had noticed for sale when he interviewed to teach biology at East Texas Baptist University. As we headed back to our car after viewing the house, Pam Dowd, the owner, stepped out onto the porch.

"Excuse me," she called, causing us to stop and turn around. We waited. She began again rather sheepishly. "I know this sounds crazy, but do you by any chance know anyone who would be interested in teaching junior-high English?" Pam was the administrator at Trinity Episcopal School, a local private school adding a seventh-grade class for the first time in the coming fall.

Her question amused me. We didn't know anyone in Marshall, period! George and I looked at each other without speaking.

I turned back to Pam. "I'm certified to teach secondary English, but I was planning to home-school my kids this year until we have a chance to check out our educational options."

Pam's jaw dropped. "Would you come and look at our school?"

I smiled at her enthusiasm. "OK. When should I come by?"

Pam later told me God had all but pushed her out the door to ask us that question. In her mind, I was the teacher she had been looking for all summer. She invited me to come to her office the next day. In one afternoon I found a job, an excellent school for the kids, and a true friend.

Pam Dowd's red-headed twin daughters were Jacob's age and would be in his sixth-grade class when school started two weeks later. A fun-loving extrovert, Abigail entertained Jacob. He loved being around her. But it was Natalie, the more reserved twin, who became one of his best friends.

As our children bonded, Pam and I grew closer, too. We sailed along in happy ignorance of coming storms. For the next four years, the waters were calm.

The ICU waiting room remained a busy place. Many caring friends came by every day to pray or offer words of encouragement. Pam and

Natalie Dowd put their own lives on hold, staying by our sides for hours each day, proving their love by their presence.

Though the body of Christ is mystical in concept, in practical matters it becomes tangible and organic, plunging in and getting its fingernails dirty. Men in our church organized themselves into an all-night sitting service, enabling George and me to go home and sleep. Every night, men sat with Jacob in shifts, ready to notify hospital staff if he went into a seizure or in any way required attention.

Women organized teams to provide meals for us. A few women offered to come clean our house and take care of neglected chores. Others sat by the phone in the ICU waiting room, fielding the endless stream of calls we received. They carried life's daily burdens, allowing us to devote ourselves to Jacob.

Jacob's friends drew posters with encouraging messages, and we used them to paper his hospital room walls. Devoted doctors, nurses, and therapists amazed us with the depth of their caring. I marveled at their ability to remain patient and kind-hearted while working in such a stressful environment.

During those first days, we sensed God's undercurrent moving. Ripples reached the people God wanted involved, and they responded. Janet Newsome, a local nurse, brought in a physical therapist to assess Jacob's needs and recommend measures for preventing irreparable damage to his body.

The therapist suggested a mechanical air mattress with side-to-side rolling motion to keep Jacob from developing bedsores. She also instructed us to use ankle-high shoes to prevent the possibility of his feet becoming fixed in a dropped position. I don't know who provided it, but the mattress appeared. George brought in his own hiking boots, causing some raised eyebrows among visitors who saw them sticking out from under the covers.

Nurses had been feeding Jacob a thick, green liquid through a small tube threaded through his nose, down his throat, and into his stomach. Doctors told us the tube in his nose would have to be removed, and the best option for long-term sustenance would be the insertion of a permanent feeding tube into Jacob's stomach.

As with the tracheotomy, I winced at the obvious meaning behind this surgery. In my heart, I still hoped Jacob would make a quick and miraculous recovery. Why fill his body with holes? But they performed the gastrostomy, and again I consoled myself with the thought that, if Jacob got well, it was only a scar.

Though a week had passed since Jacob entered the hospital, he showed no signs of regaining consciousness. His doctors contacted a neurologist who agreed to come from a nearby town for consultation.

A portly man carrying an old-fashioned doctor's satchel, his quaint appearance amused us even in our current situation. The neurologist examined Jacob, looked at his brain scans, and in a cheerful, matter-of-fact manner said, "There's really no way to know, but often people as young as Jacob recover completely from such injuries. Their brains are still growing and are amazingly resilient." He chuckled. "I've seen kids wake up from coma and walk back into the hospital to visit the people who never thought they had a chance."

This was by far the best news we'd heard, and it lifted our spirits. But for every hopeful prediction, we received several dire ones. The worst was yet to come.

CHAPTER 4

DEEP WATERS

Many are saying of my soul, "There is no deliverance for him in God."

—Ps. 3:2

In some important ways, Jacob stabilized during those first two weeks in ICU, but he remained in a coma. Gradually weaned from the respirator, he breathed without assistance. A slight case of pneumonia in one lung responded to treatment. With each improvement, our hopes rose. Doctors and therapists suggested possibilities for the next step. One thing was clear: Jacob would require services outside Marshall.

Many decisions loomed. We often felt overwhelmed and afraid, clueless about how we should proceed. We prayed for guidance, but we wondered how God could make the path clear. Then Jimmy Day showed up.

A college friend and George's former roommate, Jimmy was a surfer-turned-heart-surgeon, who took time off from his demanding schedule in Little Rock, Arkansas, to visit. He arrived wearing sandals, jeans, and a white cotton shirt—his tanned skin and longish blond hair reminiscent of former days. From the corner of Jacob's ICU room, Jimmy watched the comings and goings of hospital staff and Jacob's visitors.

Noticing his contemplative expression, I asked what he was thinking. His answer would be echoed in days to come, like a musical canon, sung by different voices but containing the same basic theme.

"There's something very beautiful going on here." Jimmy paused as though gathering his thoughts. "You guys probably can't tell, because you're not used to being in this situation. I've been in lots of hospital rooms, but I've never seen anything quite like this. I can't really explain it, but it's something . . ." He groped for adequate words but gave up with a shrug and simply repeated, "Something very beautiful."

I treasured his words in my heart. *Please, God, let there be something beautiful in this.*

Having received his surgical training at Baylor University Medical Center in Dallas, Jimmy knew about a specialized facility at Baylor Institute of Rehabilitation across the street from the main hospital. One of two premier coma programs nationwide, Baylor Rehab offered groundbreaking and progressive treatment only 175 miles from home. It also offered convenience. If we went to Dallas, we could stay with my parents, a twenty-minute drive from the Baylor complex.

Taking the initiative, Jimmy called and was able to establish a connection and begin the process of securing Jacob a place. We knew Baylor Rehab would have to evaluate Jacob's medical charts to determine if they could treat him, but Jimmy's assistance eased our anxiety. Plans came together, and on June 2, George and I drove to Dallas for an initial consultation with Dr. Mary Carlile, a physiatrist and medical director of the Brain Injury Treatment Program.

Jacob would be transported by ambulance the same day, and we planned to await his arrival in the lobby. My mom offered to entertain Grace and Luke for the duration of our stay in Dallas. Everything seemed to be falling into place. We approached this new development with hope that Baylor's state-of-the-art treatment would bring dramatic results.

When we arrived at Baylor Rehab, a receptionist ushered us into a homey consultation room. Dr. Carlile and another staff person joined us, and we settled into comfortable chairs. After brief introductions, Dr. Carlile assumed a professional posture I imagined she'd practiced on many previous occasions. Dressed in a clean, white lab coat over a dark-colored, knee-length dress, her brunette hair framed a pleasant face with a kind but serious expression. She spoke in businesslike fashion. "I've seen the charts sent by the hospital in Marshall. Jacob has suffered diffuse anoxic brain injury. Do you know how long he was underwater?"

I cringed, anticipating my own answer. "No one knows for certain. Probably around ten minutes." I forced myself to say the hateful words, knowing every additional minute he was under decreased his chances of recovery. I wanted to believe he would improve, and I wanted this doctor to believe it, too. Jacob needed her help.

Dr. Carlile's expression darkened. She seemed to be weighing her next words.

"Jacob's injury is serious. The brain can't function for long without oxygen. If he was submerged for more than six minutes, we're looking at extensive damage. I'm sorry to have to tell you this, but I think you should know the truth. . . ."

I glanced at George sitting beside me on a small sofa. His calm features couldn't mask the torture in his eyes. My heart felt like a stone. Breathing required effort. Could this doctor really be talking about Jacob? *God, please just let this be a nightmare.* I tried to silence my thoughts and focus on Dr. Carlile's words.

"Jacob's chances of recovery are slim. If he lives through the trauma to his brain and body, you should prepare yourselves for the possibility of his remaining in a persistent vegetative state." Her kind countenance and soothing tones stood in stark contrast to her message.

Vegetative? Like a . . . a vegetable? God, this can't be happening.

As though she were reading my thoughts, Dr. Carlile added, "I hate that term 'vegetative,' but it has been in use for decades. It means that the patient does not reconnect with his environment but remains in a deep coma."

"And nothing can be done?" I heard myself ask the question with the placid control of one asking a gardener about aphids. This was our son!

"We'll exhaust every option available. We want you to know we will do our best to help Jacob. But you also need to understand what we're up against. I'm sorry."

"We understand," George said. His words sounded as though each weighed a thousand pounds. As a biologist, he knew all too well the consequences of denying oxygen to the brain. Even in his agony, he added, "Thank you, Dr. Carlile."

George and I walked down the carpeted hall to the lobby. Jacob would be arriving soon, and we wanted to be there when the paramedics brought him in. We sat on a plush sofa. I ran my fingers over the pattern on the tapestry-type upholstery. Warm lamplight formed a honey-colored spotlight on the table beside me. I stared at it, numb, wishing I could be somewhere else or even someone else.

Heart-breaking thoughts stifled conversation. But we couldn't sit still, so we got up and meandered around the spacious, elegant room, reading captions on historic photographs, examining the rich mahogany furniture, and behaving as though mere objects could hold our interest.

We could have writhed on the floor, screaming like wounded animals in a trap, displaying our anguish to anyone who happened by. But we didn't. An observer might have mistaken us for a couple who'd stepped inside to escape the heat. No one would have guessed our world had collapsed.

At last we saw the ambulance pull into the drive. With so many unknowns, gratitude filled my heart when a familiar face emerged from the back of the ambulance. It was Debbie, the same nurse who had first taken our son Luke to see Jacob in ICU. "Thank you so much for riding with Jacob," I said as she entered the lobby.

She smiled. "I was happy to do it. We wanted to be sure Jacob rode comfortably and had everything he needed."

Debbie's presence was a sweet parting gift from Marshall Regional, a final offering of support as they turned Jacob over to a new medical team.

Though I had been anxious for his safe arrival, seeing Jacob again sent fresh waves of pain rolling over me. He looked wild. His uncontrolled movements—the haywire manifestations of a disconnected brain—made keeping him on the gurney a challenge for the paramedics during the brief check-in at the front desk.

We said good-bye to Debbie, and a staff member led us to the elevator. He escorted us to the third floor, Jacob's new home.

The third floor at Baylor Rehab is a specialized unit for patients with catastrophic brain injuries. It is a sobering place.

The corridors resemble a nice hotel, with burgundy and forest green patterns on the carpet and framed artwork on the walls. But these halls run between rooms containing individuals in varying stages of coma or paralysis. "Room Service" is provided by dedicated doctors, nurses, and therapists who aim to return the injured to as normal a life as possible and to help their families adjust to whatever lies beyond Baylor Rehab.

The first order of business was Jacob's bed assignment, then signing various forms and releases. Gwen, a middle-aged, upbeat nurse with a healthy sense of humor, guided us through this process. Her kind manner put us at ease, but once again we faced unpleasant realities. We signed the donor forms allowing Jacob's organs to be used in the event of his death. We signed forms allowing the hospital to use experimental treatments. We signed them all, casting ourselves on God's intervention and protection.

Jacob shared his first room with a man in his sixties who had fallen off a roof and landed on his head. His skull had not broken, but his brain had swelled, damaging tissue as it pressed against bone. He was fully awake but confused. Being around him unnerved me.

According to his sister—his closest relative who took care of his personal needs—he had always been a gentle, soft-spoken, respectable man. Now stubborn and unruly, his body obeyed the demands of his addled brain. A vest equipped with straps restrained him in his bed, but he constantly twisted and strained to escape. He made suggestive remarks and lewd advances at nurses, who calmly replied, "Now, you know that's not a polite thing to say," as they evaded his attempts to grab at their skirts or bodies.

His behavior embarrassed and mortified me, but the nurses seemed accustomed to it. Among the common stages of recovery from brain injury are outbursts of violent anger, profanity, and obscene behavior. I realized with dread that, if Jacob did recover, he might also suffer from similar personality changes. As with every other horrifying possibility, we gave this prospect to the Lord and sought his mercy. Banishing fear and worry proved to be a moment by moment battle—one we didn't always win.

Dr. Carlile soon moved Jacob into a different room, partly to provide a quieter environment for Jacob, our family, and his other frequent visitors. But the main reason was more serious. One room on the third floor was called the observation room. With its own nurse's station manned twenty-four hours a day, Baylor Rehab reserved it for the most critical cases. The staff felt that Jacob belonged there, under constant supervision.

The observation room contained four beds. A woman recovering from high-risk brain stem surgery occupied one. Though alert, she was just beginning the long process of relearning how to do everything, from the simplest to the most complex of actions. Another bed held a motorcycle accident victim, a man paralyzed from the neck down. His prognosis was grim. The fourth bed belonged to a teenage boy, Rick, who had been in a car accident. His friend had crested a hill speeding and hit a parked car, throwing Rick from the backseat, where he'd been riding with his girlfriend. The girlfriend had died.

Before our arrival, Rick had endured several major surgeries and had stopped breathing a couple of times on the operating table, but he appeared to be on the road to full recovery. We talked often with Rick, which he welcomed. He'd been in the hospital for several months already and was eager to go home, but it became obvious to us he hadn't learned much from his ordeal. Rather than recognizing his mortality, he seemed to think his escape from death's door proved him immortal. He planned to get a snake tattoo on his chest encompassing a scar from open-heart surgery. Grieved to hear him boasting about his futile, foolish plans, we prayed for him.

I couldn't understand why God would allow a young man like Rick to recover and return to a godless lifestyle, while Jacob's chances were so slim. It didn't make sense. I thought about the past year and how much Jacob had matured physically and spiritually.

I'd marveled as my firstborn stood poised to explode into manhood, less like a child every day. I'd rejoiced in Jacob's spiritual growth. He had begun to pursue Christ from his own desire and not just because of family influence. From our conversations I could tell he enjoyed reading the Bible, studying it with his youth director, and sharing his faith with friends.

Jacob had developed a personal philosophy founded in Scripture and honoring to Christ. I wasn't foolish enough to think he was anywhere near perfect, but I'd sensed Christ's claim on his life. Now what remained for Jacob? I tried not to be angry with God's ways. But I couldn't look at Rick without thinking God unfair and perhaps even unwise.

Jacob was the only observation room occupant in a coma. Though Dr. Carlile remained convinced he would not awaken, she plunged in with all the resources available, hoping to be proven wrong. She selected doctors, therapists, and assistants to serve on Jacob's treatment team. This group met on a regular basis to discuss his progress and plan strategy. Dr. Carlile invited George and me to participate in the meetings.

George and I established a routine, taking shifts so at least one of us would be at Baylor during the daytime hours. Grace and Luke occasionally accompanied us, but Grace still avoided seeing Jacob. I continued to watch her with concern, hoping she would open her heart and talk to me.

<hr />

Months earlier I had signed up to attend my twenty-year high school reunion in Dallas, scheduled to begin on June 6, four days after Jacob's transfer to Baylor Rehab. I had pretty much given up any thought of going, but I felt bad for my friend Ellen. Her husband had recently left her and their two children, trading his family for a Barbie-doll girlfriend and a sports car.

Ellen had called weeks earlier, asking if she could accompany George and me to the reunion events. She dreaded attending alone and fielding questions about her failed marriage. An attractive, intelligent, accomplished woman, she had been one of seven top-ranked students in our class and editor of our school yearbook.

I felt a mixture of pity and anger toward her husband. I imagined he'd someday realize he'd forfeited everything most valuable in his life. But for now, he was content to pursue his shallow dream, abandoning his beautiful children and excellent wife. I wanted to support her.

George and I discussed the situation and decided I would go with Ellen to the Friday night gathering. He would stay with Jacob.

At Dr. Carlile's request, a respected pediatric neurologist agreed to examine Jacob that Friday afternoon. She wanted another expert's opinion regarding Jacob's chances for recovery. In spite of Dr. Carlile's predictions, we remained hopeful that Jacob would improve. Remembering our experience with the optimistic neurologist in the Marshall ICU, we looked forward to hearing what this specialist would say.

I returned to my parents' home midafternoon to attempt a transformation from grieving mom to the smiling, energetic friend my former classmates would expect. I'd called Ellen since our arrival in Dallas, so she knew about Jacob's condition. But I didn't want to draw attention to myself, nor did I wish to spoil the evening for others by broadcasting our woes. I put on a spunky black dress, styled my long, wavy hair in a French braid, freshened my makeup, and waited for George to call with the outcome of the neurologist's visit. If we received an encouraging report, I might even be able to enjoy the evening to some extent.

It was getting late, but George didn't call. Impatient, I dialed the number for the phone beside Jacob's bed. When George answered, he said he was still talking with the neurologist. He quickly hung up.

Finally the phone rang. The expert had given his opinion: Jacob would never wake up. He would never know us. His seizures during those first two weeks in ICU were, in the doctor's words, "the throes of a dying brain."

"I've seen many similar cases in my career," the doctor told George. "If I were not absolutely sure of this, I wouldn't say it in front of Jacob."

He offered no hope.

Devastated, I called Ellen and briefly explained the news we'd received. I said I was sorry I couldn't join her for the evening. She assured me she understood and expressed her sympathy and sorrow for us. George returned home, weary and dejected. We gathered my parents and our children and told them what the doctor had said.

It was the darkest of all the dark days we had endured since May 23. George and I took Grace and Luke into a back bedroom. We all climbed onto the peach bedspread and sat close together. The only light in the room came through the open door. I looked from George to Luke to Grace, each one's face mirroring the misery of my own soul. For a few moments, no one spoke. Then we bowed our heads and prayed.

We asked God to give healing that could not come any other way. Brokenhearted, we prayed and we cried. But even in the agony of that hour, I discerned a voice like a whisper above the roar of my pain. *God is above all. He will have the final say.*

For a brief moment, fear stepped aside, and peace enveloped me. Though everything in our circumstances screamed the opposite, I *knew* God was in our midst, working out His plans in perfect faithfulness. With all my heart I clung to this truth—a faint but steady ray of hope breaking through dark clouds of despair.

My father came to me later that evening, his eyes communicating his anguish. "I've always been able to fix whatever went wrong," he began, his voice breaking. "But I can't fix this. I can't do anything. I'm so sorry."

I fell into his strong embrace. "No one but God can fix this, Dad."

I wept for my child. He wept for mine and his.

CHAPTER 5

STORMY WINDS

*And He got up and rebuked the wind and said to the sea, "Hush,
be still." And the wind died down and it became perfectly calm.*
—Mark 4:39

We chose to believe God was in control, and we trusted His love and promise that all things work together for good. But our belief didn't satisfy the nagging desire to understand. How could good come through Jacob's affliction? And why Jacob? Why a young man who was just blossoming in his faith and in every other way? Why a kid with so many talents and so much potential? How could it be best for God to unmake all He had made?

I could see how God might use this tragedy to draw some of our family members to Himself. After all, wasn't their salvation paramount in the eternal scheme of things? Was Jacob expendable for the sake of others? I mentioned the thought to my sister Sharon.

"No!" she insisted. "I want our family to come to Christ with all my heart, but that's not enough." Tears choked her. "No. This has to be good for Jacob, too."

I wasn't convinced. How could this be good for Jacob?

Of all the emotions washing over me, anger frightened me most. I didn't feel anger against God, but I discovered with alarm that I harbored deep resentment and unforgiveness toward Jeremy. Why would a thirteen-year-old boy venture into deep water if he couldn't swim?

Almost all the other students had remained on shore or near the boat ramp. Peer pressure didn't seem to have been a big factor. By talking to witnesses and comparing notes, we learned that Jacob and another student, Jason, had decided to swim out to a bridge piling. Either Jeremy had attempted to join them, or he'd inadvertently stepped off the edge of the boat ramp at that precise moment and panicked.

Either way, in my heart I blamed Jeremy for what Jacob had lost. Jeremy's drowning only complicated and intensified my feelings. I didn't view it as just punishment. On the contrary, his death and the loss it meant to his family grieved me, adding to my frustration over his senseless actions. I recalled his winsome personality and disarming smile. So much lost potential.

Philip Jones had ridden in the canoe with Jeremy that morning. They'd talked about their faith—a conversation that comforted Philip during the aftermath as he imagined Jeremy in heaven. Indeed, that image comforted many, including me. But the next moment my thoughts would spiral back to resenting the grief and suffering he'd left behind.

Holding a grudge against a dead boy filled me with shame, but that didn't make it go away. I had never experienced such intense rage toward any person before. I knew if I couldn't forgive Jeremy, I would become a miserable woman consumed by my own bitterness.

Yet, when I tried to pray and forgive him, I couldn't. Anger rose up, pushing mercy aside, and leaving me with a serious dilemma. Dependent on God's forgiveness myself, I received it as grace freely given and undeserved. God commands me to offer the same mercy to anyone who offends me, and I was powerless to give it. Longing to be freed from my prison, I begged the Lord to remove whatever bound my heart and to fill me with the forgiveness He offers. The chains felt too tight to ever budge.

After the pediatric neurologist's devastating prediction, we counted the cost of all this could mean to our family. One by one, we laid our expectations and hopes at God's feet, believing he would give back to us that which was meant to be ours.

If Jacob lived but remained in a vegetative state, he would require round-the-clock care. Someone would have to turn him every couple of hours, feed him a liquid diet and medicines through his stomach tube, bathe him, and change his diapers. He would need breathing treatments, and mucus cleared from his trach. Daily physical therapy would be necessary to prevent painful, deforming muscle contracture. Jacob couldn't even sit in a wheelchair unsupported. Transporting him anywhere would become a major undertaking. Family vacations or outings of almost any kind would be rare, if not impossible.

We faced all this, knowing he might never again be aware of our presence or in any way connect with us. Jacob could simply become a living non-person who required vast amounts of time and attention. We wept at the thought. Jacob's loss. Our loss. A wrenching, tearing agony.

We shrank from the looming prospect in horror, but had no power to change it. If God so chose, this would be our portion, and somehow God would enable us to handle it. No matter what, we were determined to cling to the Lord. The only other option was to live in this hell surrounded by hopeless darkness.

I clung to the scriptural promise that nothing is too difficult for the Lord. Even as I groaned under a burden of sorrow, the fact remained: No matter how much these medical experts knew from their studies or experience, they weren't God.

It made no difference how long Jacob had been underwater. Lazarus lay rotting in the tomb for four days, and Jesus restored him. I knew without doubt, God had the power to heal Jacob. One word from the Lord and Jacob would be whole. This faith was given to me. I didn't stir it up or try to maintain it. It just was.

I knew God *could* heal Jacob, but I didn't know if He *would*. I knew I should ask for it—"You have not because you ask not"—and I did. Every time I prayed for Jacob's healing, my faith rose, and I stood in awe of almighty God. However, I still didn't know if Jacob would be healed. My faith didn't rest on a particular outcome. It rested on God, period.

I drew comfort from knowing hundreds of other Christians were praying. From the first day, we received amazing support. Cards and letters poured in, and the pile just kept getting bigger. Many arrived from friends and relatives. Others came from people we'd never met, people who had read the paper or seen the news, people such as Mamie Mattern, an elderly homebound widow in Marshall, who wrote promising to pray for Jacob daily and continued sending him encouraging notes. Ripples spread, and people responded.

Knowing I could never repay the kindness of so many humbled me. And yet I longed to express my gratitude in a tangible way. I began to pray God would reward those who were interceding for us. I prayed He would reveal Himself to them in ways they had never known before. I asked Him to supply their needs and pour out blessings in their lives.

I had no way of knowing who all these people were, but God knew. I believed He would honor my prayers on their behalf, even as He honored their prayers for Jacob. And I hoped to someday see glimpses of God's answers.

At present, however, I saw little beyond our immediate distress. I couldn't see any grand design. Though I acknowledged God's goodness and the faithfulness of friends, it didn't seem proportional to the pain and loss.

Several days had passed since the neurologist's visit. Grace had remained silent about her thoughts, but I sensed her torment and longed to help her. Seeking opportunities for conversation, I listened to whatever she was willing to say.

During our stay in Dallas, Grace slept in my childhood bedroom. The furnishings had all changed. Nothing looked the same, but ghosts of my girlhood lingered there. I often joined Grace in that room to talk.

Late one night, as we perched on the bed, she opened up. "I feel like all of this is my fault."

The statement alarmed me. I knew her present and future well-being depended on overcoming this sense of guilt. I tried to keep my voice even. "Why do you think it's your fault?"

She hesitated, but having taken the first step, she bared her whole heart. "The boys in my class wanted Jacob to go to our class party. You know how they are." A hint of sarcasm tinged her voice. "They all idolize him and always want him around. Mrs. Berglund asked me if I wanted him to come. . . ." She paused and looked away. "And I said no. I told her I just wanted it to be our class this time." Her words bore a tone of sorrow mixed with grim determination. "If I hadn't been so selfish, Jacob might have come with us, and none of this would have happened."

I looked at Grace sitting Indian-style on the bed, her waist-length hair draped around her slender shoulders like a cape. She was too small to be carrying such a weight of sorrow and guilt. I couldn't just give Grace a pat answer. Longing for the right words to help her see the truth, I prayed a quick, silent prayer for wisdom. After a few moments, I spoke.

"Grace, what happened to Jacob isn't anyone's fault. Think of all the ways it could have been prevented!" I counted on my fingers. "There were people all around—adults and students—who could have seen Jacob go under. God could have gotten any of them to turn at the right time and look. Or . . . or Jacob could have been sick and unable to go to the party. The adults could have insisted that the kids stay out of the water. If God had intended to intervene, He could have done it in a million ways. But He didn't."

Her face revealed the pain she felt, but I sensed she was listening and thinking. Grace possessed strong faith in Christ. She believed in His sovereign power.

Praying God would silence the voice of the accuser, I continued. "Grace, I understand why you feel the way you do, but it's not your fault. *It's not anyone's fault.* God allowed this. He could have stopped it, but He didn't. It's very important that you believe this and not blame yourself." I watched the wrestling of her heart revealed in her eyes. This would take some time.

As we sat in thoughtful silence, I realized the words I'd spoken also applied to me and my unforgiveness toward Jeremy. It's not anyone's fault. Jacob's loss was not Jeremy's fault. God had allowed it for reasons He would reveal if and when He chose to. My hardness of heart began to melt.

Reaching out and touching Grace's arm, I said, "I'm so glad you told me you were feeling this way, and I want you to let me know if you continue to struggle with such thoughts." I waited for her to nod in agreement. "God alone is in control. We can't thwart God's plan. He doesn't give you or anyone else that kind of power. We have to trust that He has His reasons for allowing this in Jacob's life."

She indicated she understood as I hugged her close. I wanted to hold her until every fear and ache subsided. I couldn't do that, but I could hold her in my prayers.

Grace and I felt isolated with our sorrow in that small bedroom in Dallas. We couldn't see any eternal schemes. But God had purposes to accomplish through Jacob's life, and He was faithfully setting them in motion through the ripples. While we spent our days with Jacob at Baylor, waters stirred on other sides of the pond.

CHAPTER 6

DISTANT SIDES
OF THE POND

Those who go down to the sea in ships, who do business on great waters; they have seen the works of the LORD, and His wonders in the deep.

—Ps. 107:23–24

During our first week at Baylor Rehab, George and I stood beside Jacob's bed one afternoon discussing his therapy. Voices in the hallway drew our attention to the observation room door, where the sight of familiar faces buoyed my heavy heart. Our pastor, Kirk Werner, and his wife, Sue, entered the room. A vivacious woman in her midforties, Sue served as youth minister at our church. She carried a large tote bag over her arm. They spotted us, hurried over, and wrapped each of us in a warm hug.

"We brought you a few things." Sue smiled, her large brown eyes twinkling under long, thick lashes. She reached in the bag, and pulled out a yellow ribbon tied into a bow. The words "Pray for Jacob" had been printed in bold, black letters on one of the loose ends.

I took the ribbon, curious to hear an explanation.

Sue became animated. "Amy and Laura Tiller came up with a plan to make sure no one in the community forgets about Jacob. All the kids from their youth group at Port Caddo Baptist gathered together with our EPC youth and made hundreds of these bows. The kids have stapled them all over Marshall on telephone poles and trees . . . including the large crepe myrtle next to the street in your front yard."

Joy and pride shone in Sue's eyes. A lump rose in my throat, blocking the words of gratitude I wanted to express. I pinned the yellow bow to the bulletin board near Jacob's bed.

"That's not all!" Sue reached into the bag again and produced a handful of safety pins with yellow beads strung on them. "The kids also made these and are encouraging everyone they know to wear them on their shoelaces as prayer reminders. Here's one for each of you"—Sue counted out the pins—"including Jacob."

George and I fastened the prayer reminders to our shoelaces as Kirk grinned his approval and Sue beamed. Then George took one of Jacob's sneakers from the small hospital closet and attached the tiny gold safety pin with its row of yellow beads. He slipped the other pins in the front pocket of his khakis. "I'll be sure Grace and Luke get theirs, too."

I looked down at the pin on my shoelace. The heartfelt actions of Jacob's peers blessed me. How many people would be prompted to pray by these reminders? I tried to imagine the influence of those prayers on Jacob's life *and* the lives of those who prayed. For a brief moment, joy banished pain, and I realized I was smiling at my shoe.

<hr/>

The Marshall News Messenger, our local newspaper, ran a story on the youth groups' yellow-ribbon campaign. The paper also printed a letter to the editor providing my parents' address for anyone who wanted to contact us. Stacks of cards and letters arrived, including many from well-wishers we'd never met. We saved them all, savoring the kindness and concern they represented.

A couple of weeks later, we returned from Baylor Rehab to my parents' house one evening for dinner. My mom had piled our mail—twenty or thirty pieces that day—on a side table in the dining room. Leafing through the stack, George and I noticed a large manila envelope. We didn't recognize the name of the sender.

After dinner, as we all sat talking around the dining table, I opened the mysterious envelope and read aloud the following handwritten letter, dated June 16, 1996:

> Dear Mr. Damoff,
>
> I am one of the lab technicians from Marshall Hospital that took blood from Jacob and ran his blood test for the doctors. At one of those occasions when I was in the room I prayed for Jacob, that God would touch him. I asked the Lord to turn this situation around so that what Satan had meant for evil, God could turn it for the good (Gen. 50:20). When I saw all the people and the church posters my heart went out toward him and his family and friends even more.
>
> So as a result I felt the Lord's leading to write this poetic prayer for Jacob. Later on I saw the yellow ribbons on the utility poles and they reminded me to finish the poetry that I had started. The ribbons asked us, the public, to "Pray *for* Jacob." And that is what I did. But as I prayed I felt the Lord was saying to me that I should write a prayer *of* Jacob. I was to write a prayer as Jacob himself would pray it. I pray that what I wrote was according to the leading of the Lord. God bless you and may the Lord raise Jacob up to total health and complete healing.
>
> Love in Christ,
> Kenneth Butts

"What a thoughtful letter," I said, glancing from one family member to another.

My mom raised an eyebrow. "Aren't you going to read the poem?"

I laid the letter on the table and picked up the second sheet of paper. Kenneth had typed the poem and made three copies, specifying one for our home, one for the hospital, and one for the church. I read it aloud as well.

A Prayer of Jacob

"And Jacob was left alone; and there wrestled a man with
him until the breaking of the day" (Gen. 32:24 KJV).
Lord, from my youth my parents did know
to train up a child in the way he should go.
They nurtured me with their sweet tender care,
and then tucked me in and covered me with prayer.
They diligently watched o'er my life as I grew,
then took me to church and taught me of You.
Yet when I did wrong, they would not forsake;
they knew thru Your love a fine son You could make.
They stayed with me through my most difficult days
and trusted the Savior to direct my ways.
But now, Oh Lord, they commend me to You,
their faith ever strong that Your Word is yet true.
They know You're the Healer . . . and doctors Your tool;
we trust all Your servants, we stand as no fool.
They're counting on You, Lord, to touch their dear son;
they know that Your power is second to none.
So along with my parents I direct my prayer
and point it toward heaven, for my Savior is there.
I've asked for so little, but now in my need,
I pray Thee, my Lord, that my voice You will heed.
Oh Great Prince of Life, I wrestle with Thee;
I beseech by Thy mercy that Thou set me free.
Like Jacob of old I contend until dawn;
I plead for Thy blessing that my life might go on.
Revive me, Oh Lord, so my race I may finish;
I ask not one hour of my life be diminished.
For all that I am . . . and all I shall be,
I pray that each moment shall glorify Thee.
Through this gift You have given, I now realize
the value of life . . . such a glorious prize.

Before I knew You by the hearing of the ear,
but now I see Thee thru reverence and godly fear.
As these tragic times now come to an end,
I've discovered that Jesus is truly my Friend.
"I am the God of Abraham, and the God of Isaac, and the
God of Jacob" (Matt. 22:32 KJV).

Kenneth E. Butts, 6-15-96 @ 7:30 P.M.

By the end, I was struggling to control the quaver in my voice. I set the poem aside and looked at the stunned expressions surrounding me. For a few moments no one spoke.

I lifted the paper again, studying Kenneth's name as though it could somehow give me insight into his actions. "This guy probably does lab work in the ICU on a daily basis. Why did Jacob inspire such a compassionate response from a man who encounters injured people all day, every day?"

No one at the table could offer an explanation. Tears welled in my father's eyes. He whispered, "That's really beautiful."

His words struck me. It was like Jimmy Day had said that first week in ICU. *Something beautiful is happening.* Something beautiful and impossible to explain in purely human terms.

As I lay in bed that night, my thoughts returned to the letter. Kenneth had said he felt the Lord's leading to write the "Prayer of Jacob." The poem blessed us, but I also felt certain Kenneth's life had been enriched by his encounter with God. How many other people would be influenced by God's work in Kenneth? The ripples would affect his world, too.

I also thought about the teens in the youth group with their yellow-ribbon campaign and safety-pin prayer reminders. What would God do with the compassion He'd planted in their hearts? Their lives would never be the same.

I knew Jacob's name had been added to prayer lists by area churches, missionaries, and friends' churches. Some of those people had contacted their relatives, and his name appeared on more lists. People around the world were praying. What kind of power would God release in response to all those prayers?

I lay awake, my sorrow still as near as my breath. And yet, it seemed a veil had been pulled aside enough to glimpse a bit of God's ways. I slid out of bed, careful not to disturb George's sleep. In gratitude, I knelt on the bedside rug and offered a silent prayer. *Lord, please continue to draw near to every person who prays for Jacob, and let them experience You like they never have before.*

As I crawled back into bed, I thanked God for hearing and answering my prayer. In spite of the relentless ache in my heart, I was beginning to understand the good God could accomplish through pain and suffering.

At the same time, I knew when I awoke in the morning, Jacob's condition would confront me once again. From a medical perspective, things did not look good.

CHAPTER 7

WAVES

For He spoke and raised up a stormy wind, which lifted up the waves of the sea. They rose up to the heavens, they went down to the depths; their soul melted away in their misery.

—Ps. 107:25–26

A few days after Jacob's arrival at Baylor Rehab, nurses inserted a central IV line in his right shoulder for ease in administering drugs. We'd lost count of the number of times he'd been stuck, either for injections or drawing blood for lab work.

Jacob had always hated shots. When he was a small child, he'd bounce around the doctor's office like a pinball, shrieking in terror. Catching him required a valiant effort, and then it took several people to hold him down.

As much as I'd been irritated by Jacob's reaction to needles then, now I would have given anything for him to yell, "No!" and run around the room to avoid being pricked. Jacob never even flinched when the needles pierced his skin.

During our second week at Baylor Rehab, George and I stood beside Jacob's bed one day with Dr. Carlile, discussing her strategy for treatment. As she gazed at Jacob's face, she became quiet, then began to cry.

"I'm sorry!" She brushed away her tears. "I never do this. . . . I don't know what's wrong with me."

She looked surprised, as though the tears had ambushed her. Somehow Jacob had broken through her barrier of professional distance.

Her unexpected display of emotion caught me off guard. An instant later, I rushed to reassure her. "No! Please don't apologize! That you would care enough about Jacob to cry . . ." Words failed me. I settled for the inadequate "Thank you."

George's eyes misted. "Please don't feel bad. We're honored."

With tears still brimming, Dr. Carlile smiled. "He's just so beautiful." Then, taking a deep breath and composing herself, she squared her shoulders, spun around, and strode from the room.

George and I stared at each other in silent wonder. There was that word again. *Beautiful!* We couldn't understand why people reacted to Jacob this way. We loved him because he was our son, but why did he have such a profound effect on others?

In spite of Jacob's low chances for recovery, the Baylor staff developed an aggressive treatment plan. Infection in his sinuses caused by the bacteria in the lake water remained a concern. George and I didn't fully realize the potential for serious damage these infections carried, but Dr. Carlile did. In addition to clearing them up as quickly as possible, she also wanted to try some experimental medications, which she hoped would stimulate brain activity.

Dr. Carlile remained convinced Jacob would never awaken. Even so, she searched for all possible ways to help him. We appreciated her professional determination and her tender heart.

Cards and letters continued to pour in. We heard reports from Marshall about the ongoing success of the youth groups' yellow-ribbon campaign and how it stirred many people to pray for Jacob. Glimmers of grace brightened our days like sunlight reflected on dark waters. But those brief shining moments soon lost their clarity, swamped by huge waves of fear or grief.

One such breaker had rolled over us when we received the pediatric neurologist's bleak report our first weekend at Baylor: "Jacob will never wake up. His seizures were the throes of a dying brain."

As his words still echoed in our minds, another wave followed on its heels, shaking the delicate balance of our faith.

Several days after Dr. Carlile's tearful episode, she approached George and me in the observation room and led us a short distance away from Jacob's bed. The look of grim determination on her face sent a chill up my spine. "Under the circumstances, we want you to understand all your options." She paused and lowered her gaze.

We waited. A sense of dread pricked my consciousness. I shivered.

Her eyes met George's, then mine. Dr. Carlile seemed resolved to finish what she'd started, but her tense expression revealed an internal battle. When she spoke again, the words came in a quick, precise manner. "In cases such as Jacob's, it is not considered unethical to deny treatment and allow the patient to die."

I felt my stomach tighten.

Dr. Carlile continued. "Should you so choose, 'treatment' in this case would include food."

I shot a glance at George's pale, horrified expression. We didn't even have to think about it.

Anguish blazed in George's eyes and his jaw was set. "That's not an option."

I looked past Dr. Carlile to Jacob on the other side of the room. His helplessness felt like a crushing weight. "No matter what lies ahead, we would never choose to deliberately cause Jacob's death."

Dr. Carlile didn't argue. She smiled, and I thought she even looked relieved. Her voice took on a more natural tone. "I had to tell you. I know it's very hard, but we try to think of what's best for the patient and family. As a medical community, we see valuable resources expended and families financially ruined, all in an effort to prolong life in hopeless cases. . . ." She hesitated. "And in hopeless cases, prolonging life is really just prolonging suffering."

I focused on Jacob again. I couldn't imagine making such a decision, then wondering for the rest of our lives if Jacob had been meant to recover. It was unthinkable. A new fear clutched at my heart. I fixed my eyes on Dr. Carlile's face. "Please, don't give up on Jacob. We know it looks bad . . . even hopeless. But please promise us you won't give up."

She returned my steady gaze. "I told you we would do everything we can for Jacob. I promise you we will."

<hr />

Several days later, as I stood alone beside Jacob's bed, I watched an older gentleman in a white lab coat enter the room. He approached the bed and introduced himself, kind and pleasant in his demeanor. When I heard his name, I realized he was the pediatric neurologist who had been called in for consultation. His dire predictions had almost crushed our hopes.

The doctor explained he was just passing through, but I seized the opportunity to speak with him. I'd had almost a week to think about his words, a luxury George hadn't enjoyed the first time.

We briefly discussed his previous visit. Then I said, "I understand what you've told us about Jacob's condition. We're not naïve about the seriousness of Jacob's injuries, but I want you to know we are not going to stop praying for Jacob to be healed. We believe God can heal him."

He smiled a sad-but-sympathetic smile. "Well, that is certainly what you should do."

He didn't sound like he believed prayer would help. But it didn't matter what he believed. I remembered how George, Grace, Luke, and I had discussed this doctor's prognosis, then cried and prayed together. I felt again the hope that had surprised my heart that night. *He isn't God, and God will have the final say.*

I smiled back at him, a calm but steady smile of faith triumphant. I didn't understand why I felt so compelled to confess my faith to this man, but it seemed to me an act of obedience, and I thanked God for the chance. I also wanted to say these words in Jacob's presence. In my mind it somehow atoned for what he had heard from the doctor's lips. As he turned to leave, I felt a deep sense of peace. My smile followed him out the door.

Years earlier Mrs. Dodson, my college Sunday school teacher, had shared with me about her experience while lying unconscious in a hospital. She said, even though she couldn't awaken, she could hear. When people came in and prayed for her or read to her, it blessed and encouraged her.

Remembering her words, we resolved to never say anything around Jacob that we didn't want him to hear and understand. We talked to him, sang to him, read Scripture, and prayed aloud for him. We assumed he *could* hear, and we wanted him to know we hadn't given up on him.

As Jacob lay there, unable to connect with us in any way, I thought about his spirit—the part of him that would go on living no matter what happened to his body. *Lord, in Your mercy, please let Jacob behold beautiful mysteries in his spirit. He can't boast or tell anyone about it, so I ask You to commune with him face to face. Comfort him in his affliction with Your awesome presence.*

Praying this way brought me great joy. Sometimes a serene look on Jacob's face made me hope God was granting my request.

<hr />

The days at Baylor were intense. Every evening we left exhausted. Even though he remained in a coma, Jacob received physical, occupational, speech, and music therapy.

When Jacob first entered Baylor, he proved nonresponsive to most stimuli: a light shined in his eyes, a bell rung beside his ear, pungent smells placed under his nose, or pinpricks on his skin. The early tests were simple in form, but they provided Dr. Chock, a neuropsychologist, with necessary data for determining Jacob's connectedness to his environment.

George and I liked Dr. Chock. A small-framed, Asian man, he demonstrated his faith in Christ in a soft-spoken, gentle manner. But no amount of kindness could soften Jacob's test results.

Based on Jacob's brain activity level, therapists focused on stimulation. They also developed strategies to prevent deformity in his arms, legs, hands, and feet. If Jacob recovered enough to control his extremities, they would be useless to him unless protected from contracture. Jacob's brain was working against him by sending destructive signals that contorted his body.

Jacob's main physical therapist, Terri, was a spunky, petite brunette. She made Jacob's posture maintenance her personal crusade. Terri insisted his body be trained to proper positions and not allowed to conform to the unnatural contortions often seen in brain-injured patients.

Even with her small frame, Terri could take Jacob through a vigorous exercise routine, because she knew how to use her weight as counterbalance. She taught George and me how to adjust Jacob into an upright sitting position on the edge of the therapy platform, his back supported against a large rubber ball. Terri sat on the ball holding Jacob's shoulders and straightening his back.

She showed us how to transfer Jacob from a wheelchair to a car, and she demonstrated how to put his unresponsive and often resistant limbs through a regimen of exercises to keep them movable.

Going on the offensive, Terri decided to put Jacob through a series of castings. Therapists would gently work one of Jacob's limbs from its rigid, flexed position. Then, when they felt they had gotten it as far as it would go, they put a cast on it. After several days, the cast would be cut off, the limb stretched and extended a little farther, and another cast put on. This method kept Jacob's arms, wrists, and ankles from becoming fixed in a flexed or contracted position.

Because he had no ability to support or control his own body, Jacob would require a custom-made wheelchair equipped with features and functions necessary to his comfort and ongoing posture needs. Terri set herself on a quest to design the perfect wheelchair.

The occupational therapists focused on Jacob's hands. They wanted to keep his hands and fingers as usable as possible, should he ever be coordinated enough to relearn basic activities such as writing, feeding himself, and getting dressed. Massaging one finger at a time, they worked to relax his clinched fists.

Once Jacob's fingers were pried open, the therapists placed a plastic cone in the palm of his hand. His fingers closed around the cone, but were prevented from re-clinching into the fisted position that threatened to rob him of any possible future use of his hands.

One occupational therapy aide, a muscular black man called T-Bone, became a source of welcome relief in the midst of our day. As he massaged Jacob's fingers with gentle patience, he told us stories. We laughed at his accounts of his exploits. T-Bone pretended our laughter offended him, but the twinkle in his eye convinced me he enjoyed giving us an emotional break.

Occupational therapists also tried to help Jacob swallow and eat. When he lay flat on his back, the swallowing reflex seemed to be triggered by the pooling of saliva in the back of his mouth. In an upright position, he couldn't swallow. Saliva filled his mouth, then poured out in a thick stream of drool.

The therapists tried placing a small amount of sherbet on his tongue, hoping the tangy flavor and cold sensation would cause a reflex swallowing response. But Jacob just couldn't manage it. The sherbet came back out in the next stream of drool.

George and I rarely stood idly by. George, in particular, latched on to any advice the therapists gave. When a therapy session ended and rehab assistants returned Jacob to his room, George worked his way around the bed massaging Jacob's hands and feet. At the suggestion of the occupational therapists, George brushed Jacob's teeth and the inside of his mouth many times a day, hoping to stimulate his swallowing reflex.

Though Jacob's involuntary movements were almost nonstop, he possessed no voluntary body control. It was as though all the pathways from his brain to the individual parts of his body had been shut down. Dr. Carlile explained that anoxia—denial of oxygen to the brain—can be much more devastating than traumatic brain injury. In trauma cases, the uninjured parts of the brain will often compensate for the injured parts, developing new pathways. With anoxia, the whole brain suffers diffuse, uniform injury. Brain scans appear normal, because there's nothing unusual to see. The brain is not bruised or bleeding. It has just been unplugged.

I pondered this information. Maybe Jacob's brain was like a computer disconnected from its power source. Maybe all the data was still there;

all he needed was for the pathways to be restored. I realized this was probably a simplistic way of looking at it, but I started asking God to revive the pathways in Jacob's brain, to restore the connections that had been cut off. I prayed God would send His own power flowing through Jacob's brain and body, quickening him, awakening him, restoring what the water had taken.

⸺◈✦✕✦◈⸺

Jacob kept his eyes open much of the time now, but we didn't know if he could see. Anoxic brain injury often results in blindness. He appeared to be focusing, but the expression in his eyes looked distant and unfamiliar. I tried to fix his gaze, to look deeply into his eyes and see if the Jacob I knew was still in there. These seemed to be the eyes of a stranger. Though we spent almost all our time with him, we missed our son.

We also missed our other children. The hours George and I spent each day at Baylor meant Grace and Luke needed and deserved more attention than we were able to give them. The thought grieved us, and we decided to do something about it.

CHAPTER 8

BALANCING IN ROUGH WATERS

The steadfast of mind You will keep in perfect peace, because he trusts in You.

—Isa. 26:3

June 30 approached—Grace's thirteenth birthday. George and I longed to make it as special as possible. After tossing around ideas, we decided he would go alone to Baylor Rehab that day. I would spend the whole day with Grace, taking her out to lunch and shopping for clothes at the Galleria.

At four-and-a-half feet tall and about seventy-five pounds, Grace looked more like a fourth grader than a budding teen. Even so, turning thirteen included the privilege of wearing makeup. We visited the Lancôme counter at Nordstrom, and Grace enjoyed her first makeover.

The glamorous technician selected products in natural-looking shades, applying just enough to enhance Grace's features without masking them. As she worked, she gushed over her tiny client's "fair skin" and "luminous eyes." Her enthusiasm eased Grace's self-consciousness.

Grace examined her new look in the mirror. "What do you think, Mom?"

Her long lashes framed unsure eyes the color of a summer sky. She was going to be a gorgeous woman. "I think it makes you look older." I smiled. "And very pretty."

Grace grinned. "I feel weird." She glanced back at the mirror. "But I like it."

I placed my cheek next to hers and looked at our faces in the mirror. Ugh. Mistake. My eyes were bloodshot. I looked so tired.

She smiled at me in the reflection, and I smiled back, sliding my arm around her shoulder and giving her a squeeze. *Lord, let her be happy today.*

The day provided a pleasant break in routine for both of us. But a thirteenth birthday called for more. A couple of weeks earlier, I had called Sue Werner. "George and I hate for Grace to be stuck in Dallas, unable to get together with friends. At least on her birthday, we want her to be the center of attention. Would you be willing to organize a surprise party for her?"

"I'd love to! And don't you worry about a thing. It will be wonderful!" Sue recruited some helpers from the youth group and planned a large party, inviting Grace's friends and many of Jacob's as well.

I concocted a story about going back to Marshall for a special concert at the church. Grace pretended to believe me. Meanwhile, Sue ordered a huge cake and adorned the youth room with streamers and balloons. As Grace, Luke, and I covered the final miles between Dallas and Marshall, a large group gathered and waited in the youth room with a mountain of presents.

We arrived at the church to find an empty parking lot.

Grace glanced around, then turned to me and smirked. "If there's a concert, where is everyone?"

In typical fashion for surprise parties, they had hidden their cars. I muttered something like, "Maybe the concert doesn't start as early as I thought." I knew she suspected a party, but we had to play the game.

Grace, Luke, and I entered the quiet church. As the door closed behind us, hooting teenagers burst from the youth room, the side hallways, and every concealed corner. The large mob—enough people to surprise Grace in spite of her suspicions—pressed around us shouting, "Surprise! Happy Birthday, Grace!"

Being rather shy and reserved, Grace blushed at the attention. But her radiant smile told me the expressions of love and friendship blessed her as much as they did me.

I hadn't seen the kids who attended Grace's party since we'd moved Jacob from Marshall ICU to Baylor Rehab a month earlier. As I watched them laugh and celebrate with Grace, a gaping hole seemed to fill the crowded room. Jacob's absence was tangible, like a dull toothache. I saw it in everyone's eyes that night. Sorrow and loss cast a shadow over the fun and laughter. I wondered if any of us would ever experience weightless joy again.

In addition to the danger of neglecting our younger children, we realized other potential hazards threatened if we didn't bring a little balance back into our lives. The chaplain and social workers at Baylor warned us that families are often destroyed by the stress long-term illness generates. Motivation to engage in life's normal routines evaporates in the midst of intense emotional strain.

Early during our time in Dallas, I started exercising again, a former discipline I had let slip since Jacob's near-drowning. I didn't have much energy for working out, but I knew it would be best for my mental and physical health. In the face of Jacob's suffering, any self-centered activity tended to produce a sense of guilt. I pushed those feelings aside, believing I would be stronger for Jacob if I took care of myself.

In the same vein, I worried about George. A servant by nature, his broken-heartedness compelled him to meet Jacob's needs almost to the point of obsession. I knew his devotion benefited Jacob, but I prayed George would be able to divide his focus more.

George and I talked about our concerns, and we stood united in faith. In our hearts, we clung to each other. But it took a while before we could enjoy physical intimacy again. Guilt over any personal pleasure, coupled with abiding pain, seemed to build an invisible barrier between us.

This, too, we chose to overcome, more because we knew we needed to protect our marriage bond than from a normal, healthy desire. We acted on a conscious determination to seek healing, and we found comfort in each other's arms.

Jacob's condition was like a loud, ever-tolling bell, refusing to be ignored. We had to learn how to listen to quieter, less demanding sounds, even as the bell pealed on. Jacob needed us, but George and I also needed each other. Grace and Luke needed us, too. We prayed for the wisdom to keep all our boats afloat on these turbulent seas. And we thanked God for the prayers of others who held us up as we navigated uncharted waters.

We must have been on the right track. On several occasions, Baylor staff members approached us to comment on our family's good physical, mental, and spiritual health. When Grace and Luke visited Jacob, the staff noticed their respect, maturity, and emotional stability. They said we were all holding up amazingly well in our ordeal.

I welcomed the encouragement and hoped it proved accurate. One frequent observation, however, struck me as ironic. Visitors, relatives, Baylor staff, and friends often told us, "You're so strong!"

Strong? From the outside, I may have appeared to have a handle on the situation by pressing on with what had to be done. But on the inside, I knew only God could keep me on my feet amid the rolling waves.

And roll they did, like the never-failing tides. Waves of grief. Waves of fear. Waves of anger, sorrow, and self-pity. All of them had the potential to crush. But perhaps the worst was self-pity: selfishness at its ugliest, disguised as concern for Jacob.

Pam Dowd visited us several weeks into our stay at Baylor Rehab. She arrived at a time when I couldn't seem to keep my head above the waters of self-pity. I knew I could trust her to love me even if I shared my honest feelings. Taking a break during one of Jacob's therapy sessions, Pam and I walked through the Baylor complex.

As we entered an empty hallway, emotions I'd been suppressing erupted. "I can't stand this! I just don't understand why this has happened to Jacob. What is God doing?"

Pam paused. Sorrow furrowed her brow. "You know God loves Jacob and your whole family. Surely He allowed this for a reason. I don't know what God is doing, but if you keep your eyes on Him, He promises to give you peace."

We walked in silence through the sanitized halls. In my head, an angry voice shouted, "I don't want to be here! It's not fair! I don't deserve this!"

I knew Pam was probably praying for me even as we walked. And I appreciated it. But part of me wanted to wallow in my misery. How could anyone expect me to take this without complaining?

Then another inner voice spoke: "He must deny himself."

I knew the rest of the message. Jesus said, "If anyone wishes to come after Me, he must deny himself, and take up his cross and follow Me."

Pam and I stopped and sat on a bench in front of a window. I stared at my hands in my lap, spinning my wedding ring with the thumb and forefinger of my right hand. "I know I need to take up my cross."

Pam sighed and leaned back against the windowsill. "Self isn't easily denied, is it?"

"Nope." I let out a short, bitter laugh. "Even if I cover my ears, close my eyes, and hum loudly, good old self will still be there when I stop."

Pam chuckled, then grew quiet again for a few moments. "A violent battle begins when we choose to take up our cross. There's a real death involved. An intentional choice."

As though I'd jumped back in time almost twenty years, I remembered lessons on the cross taught by Mrs. Dodson, my college Sunday school teacher. "Dead people don't squirm; they don't demand their own way; they have no agenda." At the time I thought I understood, but now I would have to take what I'd learned to a deeper level.

As Pam and I sat in thoughtful silence, I wondered what an unbeliever would think of our conversation. To the natural mind, dying to self sounds morbid and undesirable, like giving in to defeat or letting oneself be walked on. Failing. Why would anyone want to follow Jesus anyway? Why would I want to give up my own plans to embrace His?

But I wasn't an unbeliever. I *did* believe a sovereign God loved me and had created me for a reason. If dying to self meant entering into God's purposes for my life, didn't it stand to reason I would find fulfillment and satisfaction there? Couldn't I trust my heavenly Father to reveal His wisdom and love in both the blessings and the sorrows I encountered along the way?

Later that night, alone in our bedroom at my parents' house, I picked up my copy of *My Utmost for His Highest* by Oswald Chambers. Flipping randomly through the pages, I turned to page 42 and read these words:

> Do you say, "I am not going to be offered up just yet, I do not want God to choose my work. I want to choose the scenery of my own sacrifice; I want to have the right kind of people watching me and saying, 'Well done.'" It is one thing to go on the lonely way with dignified heroism, but quite another thing if the line mapped out for you by God means being a door-mat under other people's feet. Suppose God wants to teach you to say, "I know how to be abased"—are you ready to be offered up like that? Are you ready to be not so much as a drop in a bucket—to be so hopelessly insignificant that you are never thought of again in connection with the life you served? Are you willing to spend and be spent; not seeking to be ministered unto, but to minister? Some saints cannot do menial work and remain saints because it is beneath their dignity.

I laid the book on the bed. The truth was I didn't want to be a slave to my son's needs. Could I be content with only one "Well done"? No one would fault me for wanting Jacob to have the opportunities that had been stripped away from him, but even this desire was tainted by pride. I wanted my son to impress the world and to receive the praise of men. Was I willing for my son to live and die before an audience of One?

Leaning my head back on the headboard, I closed my eyes. *God, You don't call us to take up our cross out of cruelty. It's the only way to resurrection life. Jesus wasn't looking forward to dying, either. It was for the joy set before Him that He endured the cross. Please show me how to die to myself. If I refuse the cross, I'll forfeit the joy.*

I thought about Jesus' prayer in the garden of Gethsemane. Jesus was God, but He was also a real man. He even asked to be spared the cross if there were any possible way, but He also saw beyond it to God's plan of salvation for the world.

Tears filled my eyes and rolled down my cheeks. *Father, I don't want to spend the rest of my life caring for a vegetative son. But I'll never be asked to pay as big a price as Christ. I can't pay it. And I can never pay You back for my salvation. Make me willing to do Your will, no matter what it is.*

I remembered the voice that had shouted in my head earlier that day. "I don't deserve this!" *I don't deserve this? All I really deserve is to burn in hell, forever separated from the presence of God. But You've given me eternal life. Lord, forgive me for listening to self-pity.*

Understanding the truth and living it are two different things. I knew I wouldn't morph into Mother Teresa overnight, laying aside all my hopes and dreams, gladly undertaking whatever nasty job came my way. But at least I was learning which voices to ignore.

God, in His mercy, was taking me beyond myself and into His higher purposes, teaching me how to balance amid the rolling waves. I could choose to be introspective, or I could open my eyes and behold His marvelous work. As I learned to look for God's design, I found beauty in the most unexpected places.

CHAPTER 9

GOING WITH THE FLOW

And my God will supply all your needs according to His riches in glory in Christ Jesus.

—Phil. 4:19

When we first arrived at Baylor, we assumed they would give Jacob sponge baths in bed. Joan, a sweet, middle-aged Jamaican aide with a semi-toothless underbite, informed us in her delightful accent, "At Baylor Rehab, everyone gets a bath!"

We wondered how this could be accomplished safely. Joan invited us to watch. Rehab assistants helped her transfer Jacob from his bed onto a slightly inclined gurney covered with vinyl pads. It had a rim around the edges and a drain at the lower end.

Patient and methodical, Joan prepared Jacob for a bath by covering any casts with plastic bags, removing his hospital gown, and then covering him with a sheet. She wheeled Jacob down the hall to a walk-in shower, large enough for the gurney with room to spare. Joan took the hand-held shower head and directed the gentle, massaging stream of water over Jacob's body. We watched him relax under the influence of the warm water and Joan's soothing words.

Next Joan soaped his entire body, turning him on his side to scrub his back. She never hurried, all the while speaking comfort to Jacob in her beautiful, melodic voice. Another round of the warm, calming spray rinsed away the suds.

Joan also washed Jacob's hair, massaging his scalp. Never once did the water or soap get in his eyes, nose, or mouth. These baths provided some of Jacob's best therapy.

After each bath, Joan wrapped him in soft towels and returned him to his room. During his absence, the sheets had been changed. This whole, refreshing process seemed to cleanse our souls a little, too. We always felt more optimistic after Joan's bath ministry.

George became Joan's apprentice, learning her methods and adopting her style. We knew Jacob would have to suffer many indignities if he remained dependent, and we decided early on George would be the primary caregiver when it came to Jacob's personal needs. We wanted him to retain as much privacy as possible.

Other unsung heroes served the patients at Baylor. Rehab assistants operated according to a well-organized schedule. These strong young men spent their entire day lifting patients from beds to wheelchairs, transporting them to therapy and back, and re-lifting them into their beds. They had to be gentle and careful. They also had to endure criticism and field questions from anxious family members. All of this they performed with amazing patience, skill, and good humor.

We had our favorites among them. One tall, soft-spoken, black man seemed to possess a kind heart and a ready smile in every circumstance. Whenever he moved Jacob, he spoke directly to him, treating him as though he were as aware as anyone else. He reassured Jacob, even joked with him, all the while working around IVs, securing Jacob in the wheelchair for his ride, or taking extra care to reinstate him comfortably into his bed. On many occasions, I marveled at the mercy of these people who served the seriously injured and ill. Their compassion humbled me.

Baylor Rehab introduced us to a world we had never known before: the community of the disabled. Before May 23, 1996, we had been blissfully ignorant, aware of this world's existence, but unfamiliar with its customs, language, and occupants. Such ignorance no longer remained an option. We found ourselves thrust into full-fledged membership in a club we hadn't signed up for. We had no choice but to adjust. This world would have to become home.

Out on the streets of downtown Dallas, people went about their business. I could see them from the window in Jacob's room, walking along, talking on cell phones, carrying briefcases. I felt like an alien, trapped between the realm of the healthy—where I'd spent the first thirty-eight years of my life—and this new foreign land.

How can those people just walk down the sidewalk, talking on their phones, laughing, going to business meetings? Don't they know everything has changed?

No, they didn't know. And I was going to have to get used to it. Now we could go only where handicapped access allowed. Our world would be filled with IV poles, ramps, and adult-sized diapers. Our son would attract sidelong glances of sympathy, but people wouldn't want to look at him for long. They wouldn't want to think about the frailty of the human body, or the fact that only a car wreck, disease, or near-drowning separated them from the same possible fate. We knew what people would think, because we had thought the same things.

⊰◆◈◆⊱

Jacob's feet remained a constant topic of concern. Failure to protect them would destroy his chances of ever walking again. The Baylor staff didn't think he *would* walk again, but they didn't want the possibility ruled out through neglect. In addition to putting casts on his ankles, the doctors wanted Jacob to bear weight on his feet to keep the muscles, tendons, and bones strong.

To accomplish this goal they used a tilt table: a flat surface attached to a mechanical frame that could be tilted by degrees all the way from a horizontal position to a vertical one. Therapists strapped Jacob to this table across his chest, waist, and legs. His feet rested on a platform that extended at a ninety-degree angle from one end of the table. As the table tilted, gravity caused Jacob's weight to shift to his feet on the platform.

For Jacob's initial treatment, they tilted the table in small increments, waiting several minutes after each adjustment, until it reached about a forty-five degree angle. Little by little, Jacob's weight rested on his feet for the first time since the near-drowning. During this procedure, therapists monitored Jacob's vital signs. After twenty minutes, his heart rate had increased as much as they wanted to allow, and he was drenched with sweat. The simple procedure exhausted him.

Only a few weeks earlier, Jacob had been running, skateboarding, even completing a ropes course in which he had climbed to a high platform and jumped through the air to catch a trapeze. Now, merely bearing weight on his feet drained him. Jacob's new world. Our new world.

The therapists continued using the tilt table several times per week, gradually increasing the angle. As difficult as this treatment seemed to be for Jacob, it encouraged us, because it symbolized a possibility: Jacob may walk again someday. We welcomed the tilt-table sessions.

Though we had not allowed ourselves to worry about it, from the beginning we realized this ordeal could become a financial nightmare. Luke's one-word ICU observation hovered on the edges of our consciousness: Medical care is "expensive." During Jimmy Day's visit in Marshall, he'd asked us about our insurance coverage. At the time he said we needed to prepare ourselves for a very long, costly road.

At the beginning we hoped for an instantaneous healing—for Jacob to wake up one day and say, "I feel great! Let's go home." Now we realized Jimmy was right. Any healing we received would most likely be gradual, and many costs would be incurred along the way.

George's excellent medical insurance through East Texas Baptist University eased our concern somewhat, but Jimmy had warned that we would probably exhaust its limits with a case like Jacob's. The added burden of financial strain worried Jimmy. As a surgeon, he'd seen its effects on families before.

George and I had never been rich. Our decisions to enter the field of education had stemmed from a desire to teach, not because we expected to become wealthy. We had agreed before our children were born that I would stay at home until they all reached school age. Guiding and nurturing them mattered more to us than money and possessions.

All our married lives we had lived from paycheck to paycheck, staying within our means by living a simple life and being content with what we could afford. We had no savings or investments. Many times we'd been pressed into a corner by unexpected expenses—car repairs, broken appliances—and we'd always seen the Lord provide as we trusted Him and kept our priorities intact. Now we turned to God again. Worrying wouldn't accomplish anything. We waited to see what the Lord would do.

During Jacob's stay at Baylor, we received a letter from Jerry Dawson, the Director of the Christian Education Coordinating Board of the Baptist General Convention of Texas. Because George taught at a Baptist university, our situation had been made known, and the board had decided to give us five thousand dollars to help with whatever we needed. This generous and thoughtful gift reassured us God would provide.

Around this same time, someone suggested we set up an account in Jacob's name, a minor's trust into which deposits could be made by any interested party. We opened an account at the credit union where we banked in Marshall, and the *Marshall News Messenger* announced its existence.

The response to this account moved us. An older couple we knew, retired and living on limited resources, began depositing fifty dollars every month. Our dentist and his wife gave several hundred dollars each month. A number of people contributed—some from their abundance and some from their poverty. Even though all the givers donated anonymously, the bank sent us statements detailing the activity on the account, including names. So we knew.

We prayed God would multiply blessings to these givers. Receiving such generosity humbled us and reminded us once again of the beauty of God's ways. No matter how great the needs became, we believed He would meet them. As it turned out, we had only just begun to see how exceedingly abundant His provision would be.

Jacob showed slow but definite improvement during his six weeks at Baylor. Therapists believed some of his sounds and movements had been voluntary. However, with all the constant involuntary activity, no one could be sure.

Jacob had captured the heart of his speech therapist, Julie, an attractive blonde in her midtwenties. George and I accompanied Jacob to his final therapy session in her tiny office. Julie sat across a small table from Jacob, the soft light in the room bathing them both in a warm glow. She leaned forward, opening her mouth wide and encouraging him to mimic her simple sounds. Strapped in his wheelchair to keep him upright, Jacob seemed to be trying. His mouth opened, but he produced no sound.

Julie reached across the table and lifted Jacob's hand from the arm of the wheelchair. Placing his fist on the table, she said, "Jacob, I want you to try to give me a thumbs-up." She demonstrated, placing her own fist opposite his.

Jacob stared at her fist.

I held my breath, willing him with all my heart to raise his thumb.

Jacob's hand shifted. His mouth contorted.

Julie leaned closer. "You can do it, Jacob! Come on!"

His thumb unfolded from its fisted position. Bent and shaking, it rose slightly above his fist.

Julie burst into tears, and a huge smile spread across her face. "Way to go, Jacob! Good job!"

George and I wiped away glad tears and joined Julie in offering words of praise. What did this mean? It seemed so huge and yet so small. We wondered what Dr. Carlile would say.

In spite of the shaky thumbs-up, the prognosis remained the same: persistent vegetative state. As the time approached for his dismissal, he was still classified as being in a coma, though he had been upgraded several levels on Dr. Chock's scale. Extending his stay at Baylor would have been beneficial, but insurance requirements set limitations on how long a patient could remain in the coma treatment program. Jacob would have to be moved. But where?

He could go home, but the Baylor staff strongly recommended he continue to receive professional assistance. His trach care required the expertise of a respiratory therapist. He took a variety of medications. And the intensity of both preventive and therapeutic treatment should be maintained as much as possible.

George and I felt bringing Jacob home at this stage would prove too stressful for our family. We didn't feel qualified to meet the demands involved. Our other option was to place Jacob in a facility that provided these services. Dr. Carlile began helping us search for a suitable place.

Time was short. We would have to make a decision soon. Like we had done at every other step along this unknown trail, we sought direction from the Lord, not having any idea how He would provide it.

One of Jacob's visitors, a nurse from Marshall, asked if we had considered a particular children's facility in Gladewater, a town about forty-five minutes from Marshall. She said it had a good reputation, and she thought Jacob had progressed enough to benefit from their program. Perhaps this was our answer.

Dr. Carlile contacted them by phone, and they arranged to send a representative to evaluate Jacob and determine if he would be stable enough to fit their profile. The rep came, examined him, talked with the doctors, and approved Jacob's admission. George and I made an appointment to visit the facility.

As we drove down I-20 toward Gladewater, we prayed for wisdom. We couldn't imagine putting our son into the hands of strangers and leaving him there, but we wanted to be open-minded if this would be best.

When we arrived, the administrator invited us into her office to explain procedures and to answer our questions. As I sat in the chair she indicated, I felt an awful hollowness inside and struggled to hold back tears.

Her expression revealed sympathy and compassion. "I realize this is very difficult for you," she began. "I can't make it easy, but I can try to put your mind at ease about our program. And I hope, as you look around and see the children, you will find they are well cared-for and loved."

"It *is* hard." George's voice was gruff. He cleared his throat. "We want to do what's best for Jacob, but we never imagined ourselves in a position like this as parents."

I knew if I said anything I'd cry. I couldn't look at George or the administrator, so I tried to focus on various objects in the office, hoping to gather some insight into this stranger's heart while distracting my mind. As I let my eyes wander around the room, I listened to her descriptions of the residents and wondered if every other parent who'd sat in her office had felt this way. I wanted to know how other people coped. I turned abruptly toward her and asked, "Do most of the families visit often?"

The administrator paused and looked at her hands. "Some do, but honestly, some almost never come. Some live too far away, and others are too busy. We have children whose parents live out of state."

I got the impression she wanted to make excuses for them, but her tone seemed to betray frustration and sorrow.

As though deliberately changing focus, she smiled and said, "Let's go see the wing where Jacob will be living if he comes." She led us to the section reserved for children with the most serious disabilities.

We saw at once that the staff loved children and were committed to enhancing the lives of their residents. The bedrooms encircled one central room where all other activities took place. Clean and colorful, with large stuffed animals beckoning children to activity stations, the environment suited kids.

But our hearts broke as we looked at the children, many of them sitting in wheelchairs, their heads lolling to the side. Though the staff loved them, we realized there were just too many children for anyone to get much individual attention.

As we made our way around the wing, we noticed a number of children lying in their beds. Staff could monitor them through the glass walls, but they were alone.

We imagined Jacob in this place, lying in a bed or slumped over in a wheelchair, hour after hour, his basic needs being met, but only on rare occasions receiving an additional kind word or special care. Even if we made the forty-five-minute drive every day, our time with him would not make up for all the solitude.

George and I didn't speak much, but his expression told me his agony matched mine. After finishing the tour, we thanked the administrator and told her we'd inform her of our decision soon. Numb, we walked back outside to our car.

The sun shone in a clear, blue sky, as though happiness still had a home in this broken world. How could anything be normal? I hated this!

We headed back toward Dallas in silence. We knew we had to discuss our impressions, but heaviness seemed to prohibit speech.

Laying my head back on the headrest, eyes closed, I suddenly blurted, "I couldn't help thinking about Terri and the importance she places on posture." I opened my eyes and turned toward George. "Did you see those kids with their heads drooped all the way over? It killed me."

"We can't bring him there." George's stony expression and tone left no room for discussion. "In that place, Jacob would be alone most of the time. He would deteriorate. He wouldn't get better."

"I know," I agreed. "I can't stand the thought of it. He doesn't belong in a place like that, far from everyone who knows and loves him."

It was impossible. We were back at square one. A great sorrow overtook us. We covered the miles in silence as tears poured down our cheeks.

One thing we now knew for certain: Jacob had to be somewhere near us, close enough to allow us to be a constant presence in his life. If he couldn't be home, he needed to be next door.

Back at Baylor, we shared our disappointment with Dr. Carlile, and the three of us brainstormed for another plan. The thought of a traditional nursing home wasn't very appealing, but after what we had experienced in Gladewater, we realized we needed to be open to anything. Our yard backs up to an alley that separates our property from a nursing home. It's literally right outside our back door. We called Dr. Littlejohn in Marshall and asked him if he would contact Marshall Manor to see if they would consider taking Jacob.

Later that day, Dr. Littlejohn called back. "Unfortunately, they said they are not equipped to handle Jacob in his current condition."

Our hearts sank. George asked, "Do you have any other suggestions?"

He paused. "Well, there is another nursing home, Merritt Plaza, just down the block from Marshall Manor. I don't always get along with the administrator, but it's a good home."

"Would it be a bad situation for Jacob or for you if he went there?" We didn't want to put Dr. Littlejohn in an awkward position.

"It's nothing major," he assured us. "It's more a personality conflict. She's a rather, um, 'mannish' woman and very outspoken about her opinions. But I don't mind calling at all. If they're willing to take him, I know they would treat him well."

We hung up. I looked at George. "If Marshall Manor turned us down, it's hard to be optimistic that Dr. Littlejohn will convince someone who doesn't like him to let Jacob in." What would we do if they said no?

We didn't have to wait long. Dr. Littlejohn shared his news with enthusiasm. Not only had the administrator, Pat Wilson, been willing to take Jacob, she was excited about the prospect. Having followed his story in the paper, Pat was well aware of the whole situation, and eagerly agreed to take Jacob into the Merritt Plaza Nursing Rehabilitation and Living Center.

Relief and gratitude washed over George and me. Jacob would be half a block from home!

The time had come to say good-bye to Baylor Rehab. As much as we looked forward to going home, it saddened us to leave these people who had poured themselves into Jacob's life for six weeks. We didn't know how to thank them.

I asked Dr. Carlile if Jacob would ever be qualified to return for additional treatment. She said, "If he gets to the point where he's ready to learn how to pull on his own socks, he can come back." Her sad smile indicated she didn't expect to work with Jacob again.

Paramedics placed Jacob on a gurney for his return trip by ambulance. George and I walked alongside as they wheeled him out of the observation room. One of the doctors on Jacob's team called after us. "Take care of those feet! He may need them someday."

Those words proved more significant than he could have imagined.

CHAPTER 10

UNDERCURRENTS

The LORD's lovingkindnesses indeed never cease, for His compassions never fail. They are new every morning; great is Your faithfulness.
                                                        —Lam. 3:22–23

We returned to Marshall on July 17, 1996. George rode in the passenger's seat of Jacob's ambulance. I took Grace and Luke, driving straight to Merritt Plaza to meet with Pat Wilson, the administrator.

Once inside the city limits, we began to spot the Pray-for-Jacob yellow bows on trees and telephone poles. Each sighting warmed my heart like a splash of golden sunlight breaking through clouds of weariness and sorrow. As I pulled our Suburban into the Merritt Plaza parking lot, a large plastic banner hanging from the roof's edge greeted us: *Welcome Jacob Damoff and His Family.* Pat had been busy.

After I met with Pat in her office, discussed basic plans, and signed necessary papers, she took me, Grace, and Luke to see Jacob's new room. Not only had she asked a sign company to make the banner, she had enlisted businesses all over town in her campaign to make Jacob's new home pleasant.

Anticipating many visitors, Pat had given Jacob a private room at the end of a hall with easy access to an outside door. She had removed the extra bed and replaced it with two comfortable chairs and a small table. Through her efforts, furniture companies had donated a dresser, a nightstand, and a lamp. A framed print of Raphael's angels stood on the dresser, and a cuddly teddy bear rested on a burgundy comforter. Matching curtains adorned the window. Pat had transformed the room from a sterile nursing home environment to a haven of warmth and comfort.

I turned to Pat and tried to express my gratitude. "This is all wonderful. You've done so much for Jacob . . . and to make our family feel welcome." Tears filled my eyes. "I don't know how to . . ."

"Oh, now, I haven't done that much." Pat interrupted me in a kind-but-parental tone. "It was a community effort, and we were glad to do it." She looked around Jacob's room with a satisfied smile. Pat's commanding and firm manner told me the discussion was closed.

Dr. Littlejohn's description fit her. Probably in her fifties, she wore her gray hair much like a traditional barber would style a man's. Her metal-rimmed glasses framed alert eyes that had probably never been subjected to makeup. She dressed in trouser-style pants and oxford shirts. As we would soon discover, sometimes she even wore a tie. Pat was brusque and no-nonsense in her approach to everything, a constantly moving dynamo, business-minded and shrewd. I almost felt I should be intimidated by her, but I liked her right away and believed she would take good care of Jacob.

Pat and I were opposites in appearance, personality, and style. Yet, when the ambulance crew wheeled Jacob's gurney into his new room, I noticed an unexpected gentleness in her voice and actions, even as she took charge. I sensed Pat sincerely cared about Jacob and the other residents. Her expressions of compassion toward our family were genuine. Under her tough exterior, Pat Wilson had a tender heart.

As progressive as she was energetic, Pat had instituted a number of innovative improvements at the facility. She had renamed it Merritt Plaza Nursing, Rehabilitation, and Living Center—instead of the former Merritt Plaza Nursing Home—signifying a deliberate shift in focus. Then, proving her commitment went beyond labels, Pat had hired in-house physical, occupational, speech, and respiratory therapists to work full time, along with several part-time helpers to assist them.

We'd been unaware of this fledgling rehabilitation program when we chose to place Jacob there, and we marveled at God's perfect timing in providing Jacob with continued professional therapy on a daily basis. The newness of the program proved to be a blessing. Knowing we had just come from Baylor Rehab and would have good advice to offer, the therapists sought our suggestions on how to implement a beneficial routine for Jacob. Their openness and enthusiasm excited us.

After we'd been there a few days, Pat showed George and me Merritt Plaza's small therapy room. It contained one padded platform, some weights, and a few additional gadgets. She pulled three folding chairs into a close circle and sat us down. "What does Jacob need? Any special equipment?" Pat leaned forward with her usual intensity. "Just name it; I know we can come up with the money." She smiled and winked a conspiratorial eye. "Everyone in this town loves Jacob. Whatever he needs, some local business will donate or buy."

Understanding Pat's adeptness at taking advantage of community sympathy, we felt a little guilty. But we also wanted Jacob to continue receiving high-quality therapy. We told Pat about the tilt table. It seemed the one essential piece of equipment that couldn't be compensated for by human initiative or substitutes.

She sat up straight and slapped her hands on her thighs. "I'll get him one!"

We didn't doubt it.

Life continued as a strange paradox. We appreciated being home and having the support of our friends and church. The yellow ribbons all over town fluttered their cheerful reminder to a caring community. I often received comments like, "Every time I drive to town, the ribbon on the southeast corner of the square reminds me to pray for Jacob. It's my daily routine now to pray for him there."

We felt relieved to have Jacob nearby in the care of Pat and her enthusiastic therapists. The constant outpouring of generosity and love we received amazed us. We couldn't deny these blessings. Yet, our hearts were still broken.

Grief over all we'd lost threatened to consume us. We wanted Jacob back the way he'd been before, to hear his voice, to see him smile and hear him laugh. Jacob was alive, but we missed him. We found we could function, going through life's daily routines. But we ached.

We'd been home at least several weeks before I mustered the courage and resolve to go upstairs and clean Jacob's room. I'd been dreading it, knowing that every scrap of paper and article of clothing—everything I'd find was going to hit me like a punch in the stomach. But it had to be done.

I climbed the stairs and surveyed the situation. The same mess I'd encountered when I packed Jacob's bag before the canoe party confronted me. As a small child, Jacob had been rather tidy, but in his adolescence he'd let himself go. Jacob lived alone in the only finished room upstairs, so we didn't interfere much with his slovenliness. If he chose that existence for himself, so be it. As a result, I had a monumental and painful task ahead of me.

I began picking through the items strewn about the room. Grace had forbidden me to throw anything away. I sensed that, for her, preserving Jacob's possessions would somehow preserve his former identity. However, I realized I was going to have to defy Grace's edict when I found two-year-old receipts from a school fund-raiser on the floor behind a chair. Those, along with candy and gum wrappers and other obvious trash, went into a large garbage bag.

When I discovered a substantial stash of used, disposable communion cups, I wanted to toss them out. But Grace insisted I keep them. I placed the cups in one of the boxes I'd set aside for packing anything we decided to keep but would not need to have handy. I was willing to respect her request within realistic limits.

At some points, the project became almost unbearable. Everything triggered memories. Even those ridiculous communion cups reminded me of the way Jacob used to go around the church collecting them in a long stack before the deacons could throw them away, and how he would grin at my look of disapproval. I never understood the appeal. Most likely it had been the enjoyment he got from doing things other people couldn't understand.

I picked up Jacob's backpack, still filled with school papers from the end of the year, notes passed in class, candy wrappers, and a binder. I quickly set it aside, tears welling in my eyes.

It was a long, depressing afternoon. Many aspects of this room would have to be left untouched for a long time: his posters, his drawings, his friends' phone numbers tacked to the wall. I didn't have the heart to remove them.

Though I'd filled a large trash bag and several boxes, I glanced around at a still-cluttered room. That was all I could do for now. It would have to wait. I was preparing to leave when I noticed something taped above Jacob's door. I'd never seen it before. Hand-lettered on lined notebook paper, Jacob had written a simple message with a black, fine-tipped marker: "Today is the greatest day, and I am in it." After the words, he'd drawn three crosses on a hill.

I broke down. Sobbing, I sat on the edge of his bed and prayed for understanding, for strength I knew I didn't have, for God to reach into this hollow pain and bring meaning.

Then I heard it.

"Jacob will come back to this room."

It wasn't an audible voice, but all the same the message was clear, and I knew it hadn't come from me. I ran downstairs to tell George.

He listened with the same sad expression of resolve his face often wore these days. "Do you realize what you're saying? It would take a miracle, Jeanne."

George is a man of great faith, and he knows nothing is impossible with the Lord. He is also a scientist and understands the natural order God has set in place. Brains need oxygen.

George had been praying earnestly for Jacob's healing, but in recent days he'd shared with me his doubts concerning God's intention to heal Jacob. In his study of Scripture, one aspect of Jesus' healings seemed consistent: They were instantaneous. Jesus spoke; people were healed.

George had resigned himself. If God had intended to heal Jacob, He would have done it in such a way as to make it an obvious miracle. That hadn't happened. Time had passed. Many had prayed. Jacob had improved a little, but George honestly didn't expect to see much more.

When I was in labor with Jacob, the fetal monitor began to indicate distress, and George had watched with alarm as his unborn baby's heartbeat fluctuated. At the time he'd faced the fear that Jacob's oxygen supply might be cut off resulting in brain damage. But Jacob had been born healthy and brilliant. Now George viewed the past fifteen years as a gift. What might have happened while Jacob was still in the womb had happened all these years later. Accepting it and honoring God in the midst of it seemed to George the godly way to proceed.

I understood how George felt and why he believed as he did. But I also knew what I'd heard, and I sensed the hope surging through me was not false. I received it as a gift, not knowing how God would accomplish it, but trusting He somehow would.

God is merciful. A bruised reed He will not break, and a dimly burning wick He will not extinguish. He knows our frame; He is mindful that we are but dust. God looks at our broken hearts and gently applies His healing touch in just the right way. What I experienced in Jacob's room encouraged me and gave me hope.

But George needed his own word from God to satisfy his desperate longing and bring him peace. It came in a dream.

It was a simple dream, no elaborate plot, no drama, not even dialogue. Just a vision. He saw Jacob standing before him, smiling. Nothing was said, but George *knew* Jacob fully understood what had happened, and he was well. His smile communicated wholeness and peace. Jacob knew he was going to be OK.

George awoke with tears streaming onto his pillow. The beauty and realness of his dream overwhelmed him. He treasured it, not as a promise that Jacob would be healed in this life, but that wholeness awaited him—was assured to him—and Jacob knew it. When the same dream recurred weeks later, it was as though God said, "I want you to know and believe. I want you to have peace."

George and I hesitated to share these experiences with friends. Claiming to have heard from God can be tricky. Some theologians assert that God no longer uses dreams or speaks directly to His people. They say He used those methods in a former dispensation, but now we have the Bible as our only source of truth, and such mystical manifestations are not to be trusted.

We wanted to be careful—to love God with our hearts but also with our minds, not throwing reason out the window in favor of emotional thrills masquerading as spiritual encounters. As George and I examined our experiences in light of Scripture, we became convinced we shouldn't throw authentic spiritual encounters out the window either. God does move and speak. He is the living God and He is near.

These gentle, simple messages filled us with hope and gratitude. They didn't remove us from the daily, stressful grind, but they lifted our hearts to a place of hope and comfort, a welcome rest for our aching souls.

Summer had come and gone. School would start again soon. We'd abandoned any hope that Jacob would be well enough to return to school in the fall, but the rest of us would have to, adding to our responsibilities and the demands on our time.

We prayed God would provide the right people to spend time with Jacob. His helplessness worried us. If someone harmed him, he wouldn't be able to report it. But we also knew the less time Jacob spent lying alone in bed, the better. He needed constant stimulation during the day. We put a sign-up sheet in Jacob's room with time slots for volunteers to come and read to him, talk to him, or whatever they chose to do. Then we spread the word.

The response amazed us. Some people chose regular visits, coming faithfully each week to spend an hour or more with Jacob. Others came without signing up, some of them several times a week. We had no way of knowing how many visitors he'd have on any given day. Natalie Dowd came every day after school. Her mom, Pam, came every morning.

I washed Jacob's laundry at home, even though Merritt Plaza offered the service. Between clothes, linens, and the towels used to catch the saliva he still wasn't swallowing, Jacob kept me busy. During breaks in my teaching schedule or after school, I'd drop by to see Jacob and gather or deliver laundry. More often than not, at least one person would be in his room. Jacob's friends, church members, and even some individuals we'd never met before composed this army of volunteers.

Why would a bedridden, nonresponsive boy inspire such love and devotion? It baffled us, and our thoughts often returned to the beauty Jimmy Day had described. What was really happening here?

The Merritt Plaza therapists blocked off Jacob's therapy session times on the sign-up sheet, so visitors would know when he would be occupied. They took him to the therapy room daily and visited him throughout the day, whenever they had spare time. The schedule at Merritt Plaza was much more flexible than it had been at Baylor Rehab, because fewer residents required intense therapy. Some days Jacob received hours of attention from the in-house team.

True to form, Pat Wilson obtained a tilt table, and Jacob's legs grew stronger as the physical therapist gradually increased the time Jacob spent on his feet. He also began to make small voluntary movements: a slight turn of his head toward a sound or attempts at moving his fingers.

Every evening after dinner, George walked to the end of our block and through an adjoining parking lot to Merritt Plaza. For the next several hours he talked to Jacob, prayed with him, and they watched the Three Stooges on TV. Jacob seemed both able and determined to focus on the show. Sometimes Grace or Luke accompanied their father.

At least once a week, George placed Jacob on a special gurney and took him to a room containing a large bathtub. The gurney could be positioned over the tub and lowered into it. Merritt Plaza staff accommodated our preference and allowed George to bathe Jacob. George provided Jacob with the same pleasant, unhurried bath experience he'd enjoyed at Baylor. This ritual became a special time for them both, bringing George joy because of the ministry it provided to Jacob's body and soul.

In spite of small improvements and the hope they kindled, we struggled with having to divide our time between work, home, and Merritt Plaza. Raw emotions and physical exhaustion left us feeling unequal to the demands. Just when routines seemed to be falling into place, a new development arose to discourage us again.

Jacob started vomiting.

In order to provide Jacob's nutritional needs, the liquid diet he received through his stomach feeding tube had to be rich. He developed a tendency to vomit everything back up several minutes after a feeding ended. Assuming this reaction stemmed from too much liquid hitting his stomach too quickly, the nurses slowed the feeding process. But even when they poured it in little by little, he sometimes lost it all.

The vomiting upset us. Judging by the volume of liquid he lost, we feared Jacob wasn't getting adequate nutrition. And the mess was horrendous. Curdled, foul-smelling liquid covered Jacob and his bed. Nurse aides cleaned it up with patience, brushing aside my apologies. When they finished, I bundled the nasty sheets and clothes into a pillow case and, trying not to gag, trudged home to wash it all. Though I often did more than one such load a day, I never adjusted to the smell. The vomiting trend lasted for months.

At the same time, other developments encouraged us. Jacob rarely became sick with colds or typical illnesses. As ironic as it sounded to say it, he was quite healthy. His weight caused some concern, though. He'd grown in height, but he'd lost more than twenty pounds since the ordeal began. And yet, he seemed to be getting stronger. Even the vomiting, as unpleasant as it was, didn't appear to be weakening him.

Jacob had not experienced a seizure since the first two weeks in ICU. At Dr. Carlile's recommendation, the Merritt Plaza nurses weaned him from seizure medications, and he never suffered another one. We had prepared ourselves for the horrible episodes to return, because we'd been told he would most likely have them for the rest of his life. When they didn't, our gratitude and relief overflowed.

Though we longed to have our family together at home, we could see how Jacob benefited from the attention he received at Merritt Plaza. Many of his visitors would have been uncomfortable invading the privacy of our home, but they went to see him there on a regular basis. Even so, we struggled with a tendency to worry and fret about being away from Jacob's side.

We were forced to leave Jacob in God's hands and to trust His wise provision. No matter how much we wanted to be in control, we couldn't monitor events as closely as we would have liked. We wanted to hover over Jacob and protect him.

Meanwhile, undercurrents moved, unseen by us, but not unfelt by those God chose to involve in His plan. God doesn't always allow us to observe what He is doing. Sometimes He waits for us to get out of His way.

CHAPTER 11

THE CHANGING TIDES

I would have despaired unless I had believed that I would see the
goodness of the LORD in the land of the living. Wait for the LORD;
be strong, and let your heart take courage; yes, wait for the LORD.
                                        —Ps. 27:13–14

"Come in here! I want you to see something!" Kathy Butler, the speech therapist, stopped me in the hall on my way toward Jacob's room one autumn afternoon. She led me to the therapy room. Strapped to the tilt table, Jacob stood up completely straight. Most of the Merritt Plaza therapists were present, cheering Jacob on. After several weeks of intense exercise, his legs and feet had gained significant strength and stability. We'd also noticed a marked decrease in involuntary movement.

I smiled up at him. "Wow, Jacob! You're doing great!" I studied Jacob's face. Was it my imagination, or did he look proud of himself?

During one of their daily sessions, the therapists brought in a free-standing, full-length mirror. Jacob's instant and dramatic response to his own reflection fascinated them. From that day on, they placed the mirror in front of Jacob when they took him through his exercises.

The first time they demonstrated the use of the mirror to me, I wondered if Jacob would be alarmed by his altered appearance—the weight loss, awkward movements, and lack of body control. He didn't appear to be. The mirror almost seemed to serve as a connection with himself.

He became his own motivator. The indisputable reaction to his reflection also proved Jacob could focus with his eyes and see clearly, a fact we had not firmly established before.

Jacob still had not mastered voluntary swallowing. When we placed him in an upright position, we had to keep a towel handy to catch his saliva. His trach provided easy access to his throat in case he choked. A Velcro collar worn around his neck held it in place.

One morning I received a phone call at work from Pat Wilson. "I'm sorry to bother you," she began. "We have a little situation over here. Jacob's trach slipped out during the night."

I knew Pat had been all for removing the trach, so I wasn't surprised to hear subdued excitement in her voice.

Pat continued. "By the time the nursing staff discovered it, the hole was closed too much to get it back in. I need to know if you want me to call the doctor and schedule surgery to replace it." She paused. "Or just leave it out."

"I'll be right over." Before leaving the school, I called George, repeated Pat's message, and told him I'd call again after I saw Jacob and talked to the doctor.

When I arrived, Pat was waiting for me, and we headed to Jacob's room. He looked comfortable resting in bed with a gauze bandage over his throat.

Pat immediately voiced her vote for leaving the trach out. "He never has choked, and maybe if we get rid of the trach, he'll start swallowing." She sounded eager.

Even in my concerned state, I couldn't help enjoying Pat's enthusiasm. She was right. Jacob hadn't choked. His swallowing reflex worked; he just couldn't manipulate the muscles in his mouth to manage the saliva. He swallowed fine when lying on his back.

I called our doctor for advice, but after discussion, he left the decision to George and me. Dr. Littlejohn expected Jacob would do fine without the trach, but couldn't offer any guarantees.

I prayed silently. *OK, Lord, maybe this is Your timing. Maybe You did what we were too afraid to do. Please help us be wise!*

I called George. After hearing my report, he said, "Maybe this is God's timing." The same words I had prayed. Without much discussion, we decided to leave it out. No further action was required. The hole would finish closing on its own. Though I felt a little nervous, I also rejoiced. The trach's removal represented one more step away from medical dependency.

Pat Wilson didn't try to hide her excitement.

"I bet you snuck in here and took that trach out last night," I teased.

She smiled and didn't answer, leaving me to wonder if she was indeed innocent of the charge. Pat had definite goals for Jacob and a refreshing attitude of expectancy that he would accomplish them.

A few days later, Kathy, the speech therapist, drew me aside in the hall. With an expression of awe on her face, she whispered, "Pat takes every opportunity she can to sit next to Jacob's bed, holding his hand, talking to him." Her eyes widened. "She's *never* done that before with any other resident. Everyone around here marvels over it. She just loves being with Jacob."

I marveled as well. At dinner that evening, I shared Kathy's words with George. "It's like a recurring theme played over and over again. Why does Jacob evoke so much mercy and bring out the best in people?"

George laid his fork on the plate. "Hmmm. I suppose the simple answer is that God is touching people through Jacob, but it's still pretty amazing."

"I feel so honored by all this compassion. It's not like our family is more deserving than any others."

George wiped his mouth with his napkin. "No, we're not more deserving. We have a lot to be thankful for." He pushed his chair back and stood. "Well, I guess I'll head on over to see Jacob." He grinned. "I'll ask him what interesting things he's been learning from Pat. Be back in a few hours."

Grace and Luke hugged him good-bye and headed to their rooms. I felt a twinge of sorrow at the further splintering of our family unit. But a stronger sense of beauty remained. Though I still wished none of this had happened, I couldn't suppress the overwhelming impression that God was orchestrating events. Through Jacob He was reaching into many lives, revealing His character and power. God drew near to people as they drew near to Him by ministering to a broken boy. The ripples were producing their intended effect.

I've never been comfortable in nursing homes. When I was a Girl Scout, our troop visited several facilities on holidays with handmade gifts for the residents. Some girls seemed to enjoy this and talked about it later with fondness. They astounded me. I hated being there. The smells bothered me, and some of the old people acted crazy or said bizarre things. I dreaded those visits and felt relieved when they ended.

In college I joined a service sorority. We visited a local nursing home every Wednesday afternoon. A sense of duty compelled me to go, but my feelings remained much the same as in childhood. When my grandmother moved into a nursing home after a stroke paralyzed the left side of her body, I stopped by whenever I was in town. I loved being with her, but I still had to suppress feelings of aversion when I entered the facility.

Now I was spending hours every day in a nursing home. The same smells confronted me; senile residents said and did crazy things; nothing had changed.

Except me.

As I observed the nurses and aides at Merritt Plaza, their compassion amazed me. They possessed a gift of mercy I knew I lacked and would probably never have to the same extent. But I was beginning to learn mercy. I began to see past a resident's senility to the sweet person inside. I learned to ignore smells and spills as I realized these people desired to experience life and deserved dignity. Given a choice, I wouldn't have been there. But I wasn't given a choice. God was softening my edges.

Whether Jacob's visitors felt comfortable in nursing homes or not, they continued to come, week after week, month after month. And the volunteer army kept increasing in number.

During the early part of the fall semester, George had been asked to speak at a chapel service at ETBU, to share with the students and faculty about our family's experiences over the summer. In his quiet way, George recounted details of the accident, our time at Baylor Rehab, God's faithful provision, and Jacob's current condition. A friend who was present at the service told me there wasn't a dry eye in the sanctuary.

In the course of his talk, George expressed our strong belief that interaction with people benefited Jacob, and he invited anyone interested in helping to come to Merritt Plaza as often as they wished. As a result, a number of ETBU students began coming by. Some of them had the privilege of witnessing—or even instigating—major milestones in Jacob's progress.

One of the more humorous instances involved Sunshine Gibson, a student who had begun to visit on a regular basis. Tall, blonde, beautiful, and cheery, Sunshine's name suited her perfectly. One afternoon I stood beside Jacob's bed with Mrs. Rodgers, a sweet, elderly woman from our church. Jacob lay on his side facing the window, so we positioned ourselves in his line of vision. The door was directly opposite. Perky and smiling, Sunshine entered the room and said hello.

I spoke to Jacob. "You have a visitor, Jacob; do you remember Sunshine Gibson?"

At once, and without any help, Jacob rolled over to his other side and looked at Sunshine. My jaw dropped. Jacob hadn't shown anything close to that much body control before. As excited as I felt, I couldn't resist turning to Mrs. Rodgers and saying, "Well! That shows how we rate. I guess he *does* remember Sunshine!"

What else could Jacob do with the right motivation?

The Sunshine development only reinforced our desire to provide Jacob with constant stimulation. Another encouraging milestone involved Jacob's buddy Paul Kent and Luke. They loved entertaining Jacob. In their hands, stuffed animals became puppets speaking in goofy voices and performing slapstick routines on the bed rail.

One day, as several visitors stood watching, the boys were on a roll, playing off each other and the encouragement of the crowd. Paul made a stuffed green frog fall clumsily from the rail onto Jacob's bed, adding clunky, cartoonish sound effects.

Jacob laughed.

The boys froze, and everyone in the room stared in stunned silence. Coming to my senses, I blurted, "No! Don't stop!"

Silliness had been replaced by joy and awe, but the boys continued the performance, and Jacob laughed—real, delightful, musical laughter. It was the first time he had shown any emotion. We were all ecstatic!

After that day, Luke became designated jester, coming often to amuse Jacob. When Jacob laughed, happiness washed over anyone else present. It almost seemed chains had been broken and joy had been set free.

Always on the alert for any indication Jacob was connecting in normal ways with his environment, the laughter provided a huge leap forward in our minds. Another such breakthrough came one afternoon when Karen Mayo and her daughter, Charla, came by to sing for Jacob. Both gifted with beautiful voices, they enjoyed singing together and liked to come and minister in a way that suited their abilities.

As they stood beside his bed singing a Christian hymn in perfect harmony, Jacob began to weep. Again, the stunned reaction was to stop; and again, I said, "No! Don't stop!"

They picked up where they'd left off, glancing at me with expressions of concern that they were causing Jacob pain. I nodded and encouraged them on with my eyes, not wanting this opportunity to be lost.

As I watched Jacob cry—sobs that seemed to well up from the depths of his soul—I imagined this must be a tremendous release for him. He'd been through so much in the past few months with no outlet for expressing his pain or sorrow.

Karen and Charla continued to sing. As long as they sang, Jacob wept. I cried with him—tears of gratitude for this gift that, in its own way, was every bit as precious as the gift of laughter.

Because he was a school-aged youth, Texas law provided for Jacob to have a homebound teacher. However, the law applied only if he were considered well enough to benefit from the service.

I plowed through the necessary meetings and paperwork, a process not without painful moments. The MISD director of Special Education

Services told me Jacob didn't qualify, because he was officially listed as being in a persistent vegetative state. I explained that Jacob had been slowly emerging from coma and had made documented progress, but the state needed a doctor's verification.

Dr. Valarie Allman, one of the Marshall Hospital doctors who had treated Jacob in ICU, had become his primary physician upon our return to Marshall from Baylor Rehab. I went to her for the necessary statement regarding Jacob's current status.

It had been a while since she had examined Jacob. Basing her opinion on the charts sent from Baylor, Dr. Allman was reluctant to acknowledge any change in his condition or prognosis. I tried to subdue my frustration as I encouraged her to come and see what was happening at Merritt Plaza.

She came by for a visit. After observing the subtle-but-undeniable evidence that Jacob was indeed connecting with his environment, Dr. Allman verified his qualification for state-provided instruction.

As a result, a young teacher named Julie McRight began coming to Jacob's room once a week for an hour or two. The prospect of yet another professional working with Jacob thrilled us. From the start, Julie demonstrated enthusiasm and a determination to make the most of her time with Jacob. Her efforts more than paid off.

By this time, Jacob could respond to a request to turn his head and focus his eyes on an object. Wanting to discover how much Jacob knew, Julie brainstormed for ways to obtain feedback using his limited abilities. After experimenting with several methods, she had a brilliant idea. She wrote the names of various items in the room on index cards. Then she held a card in front of Jacob and asked him to look at the object named.

The card said *window*.

Jacob shifted his eyes and looked at the window.

Julie waited, but he kept his eyes on the window. "Good job, Jacob! Now look at this card." She held up a card with the word *lamp*.

Jacob turned his eyes toward the lamp on the table beside him.

Card after card, Jacob looked at the correct object.

He could read!

This discovery rekindled many hopes we had come close to abandoning. If Jacob could still read, perhaps vast quantities of knowledge remained trapped in his brain. The question was how to reconnect his brain and body. No one knew for sure, but everyone plunged in with a fresh determination to find answers.

The Merritt Plaza therapists were among the most diligent soldiers in the crusade to help Jacob, and their current top priority was for Jacob to walk. The tilt table had served well in getting Jacob back on his feet. He could now stand on the floor unassisted and maintain his balance for a minute or two, always with someone right beside him to support him if he started to fall. He couldn't walk yet, but standing alone brought him one step closer to that goal.

In the evening, when Jacob was lying on his back, we played a game to help him develop leg coordination. We tossed a beach ball from the foot of the bed, and Jacob kicked it back at us with his feet. He could manipulate his legs when lying down, but not with any weight on them. All of his voluntary movements were jerky and uncertain. But every little improvement provided fresh encouragement. Jacob became quite proficient at the beach-ball game. He played with serious determination, yet burst into laughter when the ball shot beyond our reach.

Whenever three of the therapists could be spared, they got Jacob up on his feet. Two supported him from the sides, and one manually lifted and placed his feet, one after the other, walking him across the room or in the hall. Natalie Dowd became a willing assistant in this process during her afternoon visits.

At first, Jacob couldn't initiate any part of the walking motion. He grew tired quickly. His body position was awkward, his gait cumbersome. He had no sense of balance or control. But the therapists found that placing the mirror in the hallway and letting Jacob work his way toward it seemed to help motivate him. Some days they spent hours teaching Jacob to walk.

Jacob received many more hours of therapeutic attention than would have been possible in an environment less personal or intimate. He was like everyone's son or brother. Even some of the elderly residents adopted him. One sweet but slightly confused man often shuffled into

Jacob's room and sat beside his bed. I found him there one afternoon when I arrived for a visit.

A nurse entered the room close on my heels. She took the man's arm to escort him out. "Come along, now. Let's go back to your room for some rest."

He looked up from his position in the chair beside Jacob's bed and spoke in a soft, shaky voice. "I had to sit with the baby."

The nurse helped him stand. She turned to me and winked. "Whenever we need to find him, we know where to look. He loves to 'sit with the baby.'"

I watched them leave, then looked down at Jacob, asleep in his bed. He had no idea he provided this man with a sense of purpose. By Jacob's passive, nonjudgmental acceptance of all the ministries offered to him, he became an instrument in God's hand. His needs allowed all kinds of people to give and, in giving, to be blessed. The thought seemed particularly beautiful to me.

The ever-active Pat Wilson had not been idle. Her current project involved the opening of a previously closed wing in the nursing home to be used for rehabilitation services. Because Jacob had been such an inspiration to everyone there, Pat chose an official name for the wing: the Jacob Damoff Rehabilitation Center.

Never one to lose an opportunity for community exposure, Pat planned a public dedication ceremony for the opening of the wing. As if that weren't enough, she invited Audrey Kariel, the mayor of Marshall, to speak at the ceremony. Pat even asked her to proclaim the day "Jacob Damoff Day."

At Pat's request, we provided her with one of Jacob's school portraits from the previous ninth-grade year, which she had framed and engraved with the date and "The Jacob Damoff Rehabilitation Center." Pat hung the portrait in the hallway of the wing. She also gave us a small plaque with the same engraving for our home.

On the appointed day, family members, friends, and people from the community gathered in a lobby of the newly opened wing. Mayor

Kariel presented Jacob with a City of Marshall pin. Pat provided refreshments for the Merritt Plaza staff and all the friends who came. Throughout the ceremony, Jacob sat in a wing-backed chair, smiling and laughing, probably not understanding the whole process, but enjoying the attention. After the mayor spoke, we were given the signed, sealed proclamation which read,

PROCLAMATION

WHEREAS, the Jacob Damoff Rehabilitation Center is being dedicated by Merritt Plaza Rehabilitation and Living Center; and

WHEREAS, Jacob Damoff, a fifteen-year-old honor student at Trinity School, son of George and Jeanne Damoff, brother to Gracie and Luke, likes his music, art and skate boarding; and

WHEREAS, Jacob has been an inspiration to everyone since he became a resident here at Merritt Plaza on July 17, 1996; and

WHEREAS, all of our community is praying for Jacob and his recovery, and our citizens are very proud that this Rehabilitation Center will be named to honor him.

NOW, THEREFORE, I, Audrey Kariel, Mayor of Marshall, Texas, do hereby declare November 8, 1996 as "JACOB DAMOFF DAY" in Marshall, Texas, and urge all our citizens to continue their prayers for Jacob, as well as his family, and express our love and appreciation to Jacob for being such a fine example to all of us.

IN WITNESS WHEREOF, I have hereunto set my hand and caused the Seal of the City of Marshall to be affixed this 7th day of November, 1996.

The mayor's signature and the City of Marshall seal appeared at the bottom of the page. Though her name is absent, no doubt Pat Wilson was the primary author.

The *Marshall News Messenger* sent a reporter to cover the grand occasion. A picture of Jacob, George, and Mayor Kariel accompanied the story. As we clipped the article to add it to all the other evidences of support we'd been saving, we felt overwhelmed by the thoughtfulness and love poured out on Jacob and our family. Almost six months had passed since the accident. Rather than forgetting about Jacob, more and more people seemed to be drawn into the crusade to help him.

Some friends expressed regret that they lacked the leisure for frequent visits, but assured us a constant burden to pray kept them on their knees. We never underestimated the importance of prayer. More than anything, Jacob needed healing that only God could give. If God called people to pray, we assumed He intended to answer. What kind of power would be released by these prayers offered in faithful obedience? Just the thought refreshed us and helped us face each new day with hope.

CHAPTER 12

A SONG ON THE WATERS

The Healer does not speak to us from a distance, He comes under
our roof and sometimes we hear songs or fragments of songs.
                                                —Amy Carmichael

Progress that takes only a few words to explain took months to accomplish. Even so, we rejoiced at any sign of improvement. We considered every little step forward a gift from God—a step beyond what the medical experts had predicted. And yet, in spite of these advances—or maybe partially because of them—we continued to battle sorrow, grief, and frustration.

While we celebrated something as small and simple as a laugh, Jacob's peers went on with their lives, maturing into young adults, learning to drive, experiencing all the normal adventures associated with growing up. Though they expressed love and concern for Jacob, many of them became too busy to come by often. Their lives were filled with the excitements belonging to typical, healthy youth.

I hated feeling jealous, but just seeing one of his friends drive by in a car left a bitter taste in my mouth. Jacob should have been learning advanced algebra, not struggling to turn over in bed. He should have been perfecting difficult skate board tricks, not trying to balance well enough to stand up.

A few friends—like Natalie—remained faithful participants in the battle for Jacob's recovery. But we couldn't escape the inevitable. Time marched on, leaving Jacob behind. It broke our hearts.

I spent part of each weekday at Trinity Episcopal School, where my teaching load had been slightly altered. The church had hired a new youth minister, a single young man in his late twenties named Barton Ballard, who desired to make use of his teaching credentials by taking on a few classes at the school. I had met him and felt comfortable letting him assume responsibility for the Bible classes in the upper grades. This freed some time in my schedule, allowing me to step into a position the school needed to fill: the third-through-sixth-grade music classes.

Since Barton would be teaching my Bible curriculum, I worked closely with him in the transition process. Through our interaction as co-workers, we became friends. Barton was new to Marshall and didn't know many people, so he was a willing, available listener and a much-appreciated sounding board for me.

We hadn't been working together long when Barton asked me if he could come to our house for dinner. His boldness amused me, but I was happy to invite him over. An aspect of playful cynicism in Barton's personality appealed to my sense of humor. We got along great.

One day near the beginning of the fall semester, George returned home from ETBU and joined me in the kitchen. "Guess who came by my office today?"

I continued chopping vegetables for dinner. "I don't know. Who?"

George leaned against the counter. "Barton."

"What did he want?"

"He wanted to ask my permission to be your friend."

I stopped chopping and looked at him. "What? Why did he do that?"

George grinned. "Well, he said he really enjoyed your friendship, but he wanted to make sure it was OK with me." He chuckled. "He said he wasn't asking permission to date you."

I laughed. "OK. Well, that's good."

"I told him I appreciated his coming by." George popped a carrot slice in his mouth. "And I gave him my blessing to be your friend. I kept thinking about Marjorie Griffin and how, as an older woman and mentor, she played such an important role in my spiritual growth. Maybe the Lord wants to use you in that way in Barton's life."

"Hmmm. Maybe. That's cool that he came by and asked you."

"I thought so."

We were both impressed with the honesty and openness of Barton's approach, admiring his desire to build a friendship with another man's wife only after obtaining his permission. George and I felt the age difference between Barton and me would be enough to prevent an appearance of impropriety, even if we were seen alone together.

At the same time, I realized I'd have to be careful to avoid emotional dependency on Barton. Even though I was almost twelve years older, I recognized the potential danger in our becoming too close. Barton was personable and attractive, with rugged good looks one female friend described as comparable to a J. Crew model. I loved my husband, but I wasn't stupid.

One day, not long after Barton's visit with George, I sat at my desk during my planning period. I tried to concentrate on lesson plans, but I found myself battling oppressive thoughts. Even though almost six months had passed since the accident, mental assaults seldom left me alone for long. Though I yearned to be free of them, questions still plagued my mind. *Lord, with all the rotten kids in the world, why would You choose for this to happen to my son? Why, when he was growing in his love for You, did You find it best to wipe him out?*

I couldn't find answers to satisfy me. As much as I desired to honor God with all my thoughts, I didn't have the power to hold these questions at bay.

Barton walked into my classroom just as I felt myself sinking under a cloud of depression. He sat in one of the student chairs and grinned. "Hey. What's up?"

I wasn't in the mood to talk to anyone, but I set my pen on the desk and swiveled my chair to face him. *"What's up?* At the moment, I'm trying very hard not to be mad at God!"

Barton's smile faded. He said nothing, but he also made no move to leave.

Hot tears stung my eyes. "Can you tell me why God would destroy a brilliant, talented young man who loved Him and wanted to live for

Him? Look at all the dope-heads running wild in the streets. What good are they accomplishing in the world? Why didn't God let one of them drown? Jacob had so much potential. And it's gone."

I knew I sounded faithless. I didn't care. I spewed the questions that tormented my mind, not even attempting to soften them with acceptable Christian qualifiers like "I believe God does what is best for us."

Barton listened in silence, sorrow in his eyes. He couldn't supply the answers, and he didn't try.

I sighed. "I'm sorry, Barton. You didn't come in here to listen to my ranting."

He smiled. "Go ahead and rant. We all need to vent our feelings now and then."

"Thanks." I managed a weak grin. "It doesn't change anything, but the venting does help."

I appreciated Barton's availability. I could always talk to my sisters on the phone, but they didn't live nearby. Sometimes I needed to be able to look another person in the eye, pour out all the dark venom in my soul, and still see acceptance. Barton proved himself a willing support. On pleasant afternoons, we sometimes walked the blocks around the school, discussing his ideas for youth ministry or pondering God's purposes in suffering. Barton was a new friend, but we wasted no time on shallow topics. Our relationship plunged straight into the deep end.

I saw Barton every day at work, but I also relied on Pam Dowd. As my steady, constant friend, she had walked through every step of this ordeal with me. She'd proven her faithfulness as the months dragged on. I knew I could count on her to be there for me whenever I needed her. Pam was always a phone call away.

As much as I longed to, I still couldn't bring myself to share my deepest pain with George. When we discussed Jacob's condition, the agony in his eyes broke my heart. I masked my misery in George's presence, but I couldn't keep it bottled inside. For my own health and sanity, I required the freedom to express my honest feelings without fear of offending or appearing to have lost my trust in God.

Barton and Pam didn't judge me for my human weakness. They helped me find my way back to victorious faith, and I couldn't have stood without them. They were like Aaron and Hur, who supported

Moses' hands during Israel's battle against Amalek, lest he grow weary and his hands fall and Israel be defeated. In my battle against anger, frustration, and self-pity, Pam and Barton were Aaron and Hur for me.

As I thought about how much I relied on them, I better understood why Scripture calls believers "the body of Christ." No one member stands alone. God never intended any one of His children to endure life's difficult battles unaided. In the months that followed Jacob's near-drowning, God provided many friends to come alongside our family as comrades, weeping and suffering with us, standing with us in the battle.

Prayer was the glue that held everything together. So many people prayed, it seemed like a cloud of intercession enveloped us, going before us, hovering over us, watching our backs. We felt it. We leaned on it. We stood in humble, grateful awe of the power of God it released into our lives. We never took it for granted.

In the only way I could repay all the people who prayed for us, I had continued asking God to bless and draw near to each one of these intercessors as they bowed before Him on Jacob's behalf. I prayed believing He would answer, and it brought me joy.

One afternoon I received a phone call from Debbie Boatright-Camacho. She introduced herself as an ETBU student in one of George's classes and said she had written a song for Jacob. She'd sung it for George, and he had encouraged her to call me, assuring her that I would love to hear it.

I invited her to come over that afternoon. Debbie arrived, guitar in hand, a petite brunette with an infectious grin and a quaint Texas accent. We sat in the living room, and she explained the story behind the song she was about to sing.

Debbie had returned home one recent evening to a messy house, kids in need of attention, and a myriad of other responsibilities. She'd planned to spend some time in prayer for Jacob. In fact, she had felt a particularly strong urge to pray, but the clutter and chaos distracted her. She almost abandoned the idea of praying, but even as she considered it, the burden returned with intensity.

Choosing to ignore immediate demands for at least a few moments of prayer, Debbie lay on the floor with her face to the carpet. As she prayed, tears began to flow, and the words to a song filled her mind. She snatched a scrap of paper and a pencil and jotted down the verses as though she were taking dictation.

Sitting in my living room, Debbie picked up her guitar and sang for me what she had written that night, words that had seemed to issue not from her own mind, but through it. In her sweet, soothing alto, Debbie sang what was almost a lullaby.

Jacob's Song

Sometimes there's just no way to explain it all;
And we question: Lord, why is this the path that I must walk?
Though the shadows fall across our way,
We must know that there's a better day—

He's the healer, He's the keeper, He's the One who makes it all.
And when you get to the end of your rope, Just let go and fall,
For His arms will catch it all.

Remember a special time of peace from days ago,
Now imagine a greater peace than you have ever known.
This peace awaits your soul;
We only must let go—

He's the healer, He's the keeper, He's the One who makes it all.
And when you get to the end of your rope, Just let go and fall,
For His arms will catch it all.

Still yet we hope and pray and we watch for signs;
But we know in our own hearts is where the healing lies.
There is more God wants to say;
That is why He remolds the clay—

He's the healer, He's the keeper, He's the One who makes it all.
And when you get to the end of your rope, Just let go and fall,
For His arms will catch it all.

He's my healer, He's my keeper, He's the One who makes it all.
And when I get to the end of my rope, I'll let go and fall
For His arms will catch it all, For His arms will catch us all.

As she sang I was struck with a sense not only of the song's beauty, but of its importance. Debbie flashed a shy smile at me as she finished. I leaned forward, my elbows resting on my knees, my eyes on Debbie's face. "Will you teach me this song? I really want to know it. I love it! It's beautiful, and it says exactly what so many people need to hear."

I wrote the words on a sheet of paper as she repeated them. Then I penciled in the chords, got my guitar, and had her sing it again. As I learned the song, I added harmonies. Our voices produced a nice blend, and we both became excited about the possibility of singing "Jacob's Song" together.

The pastors of various churches in Marshall had decided to put together a community-wide Thanksgiving service, scheduled to take place in the large chapel at ETBU. Our church praise band had been asked to provide some of the music, which meant I would be playing piano and singing in the service.

I asked Debbie if she would be interested in singing "Jacob's Song" with me that night. Many people in the community had been supportive of Jacob and our family. I knew they would be blessed to hear this gift the Lord had given Debbie. She was happy and eager to consent, so I approached our pastor with the suggestion. He added "Jacob's Song" to the program.

When the evening arrived, people from all denominations filled the chapel. Debbie and I carried our guitars to center stage. I looked out at the faces of many who'd prayed, donated money to Jacob's trust, and visited him at Merritt Plaza. A lump of gratitude rose in my throat.

"I want to thank all of you for praying with our family since Jacob's near-drowning. God is answering your prayers. Jacob has improved beyond all medical expectations, and tonight he's here with us."

I smiled and gestured toward Jacob in his wheelchair. "Debbie and I are going to share a song the Lord gave her as she prayed for Jacob one evening. She calls it 'Jacob's Song,' but if you are suffering tonight, this song is for you, too."

Then Debbie and I sang. We both played guitar, a soft finger-picking accompaniment to the lovely, haunting melody.

I'm not sure how I managed to make it through without crying. Most of the people present wept openly. But the tears didn't indicate sadness. They were tears of affirmation—of understanding that, though life can be terribly painful, God abides above it all, unshaken and unmoved. And He is our keeper.

After that night, when I found myself sinking back into depression, I often sat alone at the piano in our living room and sang the song as both a prayer and a reminder. With no one but the Lord in the audience, I let the tears flow unhindered down my cheeks. "There is more God wants to say. That is why He remolds the clay."

"Jacob's Song" had set more ripples in motion. And God wasn't finished with it yet.

<hr>

George had to leave town for a few days, so I took his place in the evenings at Merritt Plaza. We preferred that one of us be there to put Jacob to bed for the night. As he lay all tucked in one evening, his teeth brushed and his face washed, I sat beside him on a stool, gazing at him with a mixture of emotions. He *was* beautiful. And without the trach, lying there with his eyes closed, he looked as though he could open them at any moment and say, "Hey, Mom, what are we doing in this place? Let's go home!"

The dull heartache I had learned to live with pressed itself upon my consciousness. Sighing, I leaned over to pray for Jacob before turning off the light and going home to leave him to a night's rest. I placed the palm of my hand on the side of his face. As I did, he pressed his face against my hand, almost like a caress, his eyes still closed. His expression relaxed. Peace written on his face.

My heart melted as tears sprang to my eyes. *Oh Lord, how many fifteen-year-old boys respond so sweetly to their mother's touch? Let me receive gifts like this with the gratitude they deserve. Thank You that Jacob is still here, still my son, still in my life.* Then I prayed aloud for Jacob—for

God to accomplish His will in his life, that by His power He would bring to pass every good word He had spoken concerning Jacob, every single plan He had ordained. I prayed that not one opportunity would be lost.

Jacob was a patient prayer partner.

I prayed a long time.

CHAPTER 13

SLOW, STEADY RIPPLES

The LORD is the one who goes ahead of you; He will be with you.
He will not fail you or forsake you. Do not fear or be dismayed.
—Deut. 31:8

Jacob received amazing benefits from intense therapy and constant stimulation. We felt deep gratitude for the progress he was making, but dividing our time and energies between home and Merritt Plaza placed unavoidable strain on our family. George worked all day at ETBU, came home, ate dinner, interacted briefly with Grace and Luke, and then left to spend the evening with Jacob.

Sometimes one or both of the kids went along, but most days they remained at home engaged in their own activities. Because I taught at the school Grace and Luke attended, brought them home in the afternoons, and stayed with them in the evening, I felt they received enough attention from me to satisfy their desires and needs. But they spent much less time with George than they had before Jacob's accident.

I knew they both understood their father's dedication to Jacob, but I also knew they missed his presence and influence. All I could do was ask the Lord to cover them with His protection and keep them from emotional or psychological harm.

As Christmas approached, George and I longed to make it as much a family occasion as possible. In early December, we began bringing Jacob home for several hours at a time, pushing his wheelchair the short distance from Merritt Plaza to our house. The first time we wheeled him up the steps was a bittersweet moment. We couldn't tell what he felt or remembered, but just having him back at home after so many months filled us with joy.

During one of these visits, we positioned an armchair in front of our Christmas tree and sat Jacob in it. The rest of us gathered around him and, using our camera's timer, snapped a family portrait to send out with our annual Christmas letter.

My tradition in the past had been to write a one-page, humorous review of our year—hitting the highlights, while making it obvious we try not to take ourselves too seriously. This year I would have to rethink my strategy. Some of the people who received this letter would learn of Jacob's near-drowning for the first time. I couldn't leave such important information out, but I didn't want to dump alarm and sorrow on everyone's Christmas platter.

The family picture turned out great. Our expressions, including Jacob's, radiated joy. The letter read as follows:

> Merry Christmas from the Damoffs!
> "And He is before all things, and in Him all things hold together." —Col. 1:17
>
> Last Christmas our card began with the above verse. How could we have possibly known just how much we would depend upon the Lord to hold all things together for our family this year? Jacob's near-drowning accident in May thrust us into a whole new dimension of trusting God. And we have found God to be truly faithful. Though it has been the hardest thing any of us has ever experienced, it has also been the greatest opportunity to see the hand of God at work.
>
> Jacob continues to progress in his recovery, and we thank God every day for what He is doing in and through Jacob. We know that the Lord will fulfill His purpose. We've seen Him meet the needs of our family. We've marveled at His tender care for Grace and Luke—how He has helped them to work through their pain and to keep their joy for life. They are both continuing to excel in everything they do.

We've felt His strong arm holding us up as we've ridden an emotional roller coaster. We've been humbled and blessed by the great outpouring of love from family, friends, church, and the community. God has already accomplished so much more than anyone imagined, and the hidden work He is doing in the hearts of people is perhaps even greater. Only eternity will reveal the full extent of the Lord's purposes.

This Christmas we are even more thankful for the amazing gift of God: that He gave us His own Son, sending Him to earth to bear the punishment for our sins. The love of God gave us a Savior; the love of God gives us the strength for each new day; the love of God fills us with peace that passes all understanding; the love of God is restoring our son to us—all at the cost of His Son's life. We stand in awe of our generous loving God, and we pray that you are knowing and experiencing the same sense of joy and amazement this Christmas. May you see the King in His beauty, and may your heart rejoice!

Only seven months had passed since the May 23 accident, but this letter reveals our awareness of the ripple effect. By faith we were able to proclaim that God's purposes—greater and more far-reaching than we could imagine—were being fulfilled.

Every Christmas since we married, George and I had traveled to one of our parents' homes and spent the holidays with them and other relatives. We alternated years between his family and mine. Under normal circumstances, we would have been going to see George's family in Florida this year, a two-day drive that we often broke up by spending the night at his brother's house in Mobile, Alabama.

George approached me as I sat reading the newspaper in the dining room one evening. "I think we should still go to Florida." Before I could respond he added, "And I think we should take Jacob."

I looked up at him. "Can Jacob handle a trip like that?"

He sat beside me. "We'll take it slow . . . stop often. He'll be fine."

I'd seen that look and heard the tone before. George can be a determined man. I smiled at him. "Pat Wilson isn't gonna like this."

He grinned back. "I guess she'll just have to get used to the idea."

We began considering what it would take to include Jacob on a long road trip. My parents had financed the purchase of a full-sized Ford Econoline van equipped with a ramp. Removal of a rear captain's seat created space for the wheelchair. However, since the time of its purchase, Jacob had gained enough strength and balance that George could assist him into the original seat. We wouldn't need the ramp or the wheelchair.

In spite of this positive development, many other variables had to be taken into consideration. Merritt Plaza could provide us with enough diapers and canned liquid food to last the ten days we'd be gone. We would also need a supply of Jacob's medications. George and I had both fed Jacob many times through his stomach tube, and George remained the uncontested pro at bathing him. We were also well practiced and comfortable with all the other necessary personal care activities.

With a thorough plan in place, we approached Pat Wilson. Though her protective instincts were strong when it came to Jacob, we convinced Pat we could manage it. She admitted the trip sounded like it would be a positive experience for Jacob and our family.

After making all the arrangements, we loaded the van, prayed together as a family, and headed east. Excitement conquered anxiety. We were determined to overcome any challenges we faced in this new adventure. Remembering our sorrow at the prospect of never being able to go anywhere again as a family, we thanked God we were at least being given the chance to try.

Jacob traveled well most of the time, but we encountered some expected difficulties. The road afforded limited privacy. When Jacob needed a fresh diaper, we pulled over and stopped, all of us got out, and George positioned Jacob on his back on the floor of the van to take care of his needs. Then we climbed back into the van and continued on. Progress was slow.

After one of his liquid meals, Jacob vomited in the van. The mess required an extensive clean-up process and left us with a garbage bag full of smelly, soiled laundry. Thankfully, we'd brought along a supply of large, waterproof pads for Jacob's car seat, and he only vomited once.

These unpleasant inconveniences tested our patience, but we pressed on, reminding ourselves how blessed we were to be on the road at all.

Some of the relatives who gathered for Christmas in Florida that year hadn't seen Jacob since his accident. Even though they'd followed the reports of his progress, seeing him in his altered state required some initial adjustment. But gratitude remained the overriding emotion. Jacob was still a part of the family. He'd been able to travel halfway across the nation and appeared none the worse for it. The whole family pitched in to do whatever they could to accommodate Jacob's needs.

When we returned to Marshall, we took Jacob back to Merritt Plaza. His arrival created quite a stir. Pat, the staff, and even a few residents welcomed Jacob like a long-lost brother. The affectionate reception pleased and amused us, but the trip to Florida had planted a new seed in our minds. If we could manage for more than a week on the road and in a regular house, maybe it was time to start thinking about bringing Jacob home.

We knew he received remarkable therapy and enjoyed a constant parade of devoted visitors at Merritt Plaza, much of which he would likely forfeit if we moved him to our house. However, we began to consider the possibility and turned our attention toward identifying available options for ongoing therapy. We would have to discover ways to meet all Jacob's needs from a home base.

Once again we found ourselves in unfamiliar territory. We began looking into home health care, private therapy providers, and suppliers of equipment and food. Jacob would need a hospital bed, wheelchair ramps for the outside stairs, and an IV pole for hanging the bag of liquid food that dripped into his stomach tube through the night. He would also require constant supervision. If we brought Jacob home, we wanted his recovery to continue.

We could see how God had led us and met every need up to this point. Though we loved and appreciated the people at Merritt Plaza, the more we considered present circumstances, the more we believed Jacob should return home sometime in the near future. As with other important decisions we'd faced, we prayed for guidance and began to ask experienced people for advice.

Jacob continued his routine at Merritt Plaza, and we still saw signs of slow, steady progress. The staff at Baylor had predicted Jacob would reach a plateau in his recovery, a common occurrence with brain injury.

Sometimes changes became so imperceptible, George suggested perhaps his brain had reached its capacity for improvement. For George, scientific knowledge challenged faith to give up.

But faith would not bow to any prognosis. God had already brought Jacob far beyond expert predictions. As much as we would have loved flipping to the last chapter to find out how this was going to end, George and I both realized Jacob's recovery no longer fell into the "normal" category. We couldn't see the future, but we believed in a God who could. And nothing is impossible with God.

CHAPTER 14

EVERY RIPPLE MATTERS

We can all see God in exceptional things, but it requires the culture of spiritual discipline to see God in every detail. Never allow that the haphazard is anything less than God's appointed order, and be ready to discover the Divine designs anywhere.

—Oswald Chambers

Jacob was walking!

With one person on each side supporting him, Jacob could now control his own legs. Watching his awkward and exaggerated gait thrilled us more than the graceful stride of an Olympic runner ever could.

Natalie Dowd came most afternoons to take him for a stroll through the halls of Merritt Plaza. Sometimes I assisted her, and we laughed at his eagerness, delighted to see him managing with the help of only two girls.

I loved Natalie like a daughter, and not just because her mother was my dear friend. I knew how close Natalie and Jacob had been before his near-drowning. She'd even shared with me that she'd harbored hopes of their marrying someday. His injury meant a devastating personal loss in her young life, making her current commitment to him even more poignant.

When I watched her with Jacob, I sensed her presence inspired him in a way no one else's could. I believed she provided him with a tangible reason to improve. Jacob loved her. I grieved over their shattered dreams almost as deeply as I grieved for our family.

With Natalie's consistent help, Jacob's balance and walking technique improved daily. Before long, one person alone could steady him.

Swallowing, however, remained a major hurdle. Jacob could keep his lips closed and hold the saliva in, but he couldn't manipulate it to the back of his throat and swallow. He still had to spit it out. We could tell by his puffed cheeks and pursed lips when his mouth was full, and we'd place a washcloth or towel under his chin to relieve him. Jacob released the saliva into the cloth as soon as we did.

It didn't take long to drench a towel. If no one was available to catch the stream of saliva, or if we didn't get there in time, it poured out onto his shirt. The only time he swallowed was when he lay on his back; and he was so much stronger now, he stayed up most of the day.

No one had come up with any good ideas to help Jacob master swallowing. The problem didn't seem to be with the swallowing reflex. His brain just didn't seem to know how to tell the mouth muscles what to do. Until Jacob overcame this obstacle, eating and talking remained unattainable goals. The closest Jacob had come to speech had been an occasional grunt.

In January, we decided to go to Dallas for a weekend visit with my parents. We had survived the daunting Florida trip. A two-and-a-half-hour drive to Dallas would be a breeze in comparison. Again we made the necessary arrangements with Merritt Plaza, gathering the required gear in preparation for a weekend away.

The process reminded me of traveling with an infant. But instead of a playpen, car-seat, stroller, and bottles, we packed a wheelchair, adult-sized pads for Jacob's seat, a case of canned food, and spit towels. And much bigger diapers.

While we were in Dallas, we drove to Baylor Rehab to visit with Jacob's medical team. We knew they would be surprised and excited to see how far he had come in his recovery. Though we still used a wheelchair for considerable distances, we left it in the car. We wanted the staff to see Jacob on his feet.

Entering the building prompted mixed feelings. The people here had been indispensable to Jacob's early progress. But vivid memories also flooded my mind of tortured days when we were given virtually no hope. Even so, we rode the elevator to the third floor in gleeful anticipation.

The scene couldn't have played out better if it had been scripted by Hollywood. The elevator doors opened. We stood facing the nurses' station. At that moment, several of Jacob's nurses and one of the main doctors on his team were engaged in discussion behind the counter. As we escorted Jacob out, their mouths dropped open. The doctor snatched up the phone and called several other stations. "You won't believe who just *walked* off the elevator!"

Word spread quickly. Many smiles—and equally as many tears—greeted Jacob that afternoon as we visited with Dr. Carlile, Dr. Chock, the chaplain, nurses, aides, and therapists. Jacob became a celebrity, bringing great joy to a group of people who rarely saw cases as critical as his turn in such a dramatic way. They did not mince words, proclaiming Jacob a miracle. He smiled and basked in the attention.

We told Jacob he'd been in Baylor for six weeks. As we walked past the door to the observation room, we glanced inside the familiar space with its four beds. I led Jacob to the door and said, "Jacob, do you remember which bed was yours?"

In quiet awe, we watched him go straight toward the corner of the room that had been his home for those long, eventful weeks. He stood beside the bed, staring at it with a serious, concerned expression. How could he be so sure, having been in a coma the whole time? Could it be a coincidence? He certainly seemed to know.

We didn't linger. Another patient now occupied the bed. But Jacob's behavior raised some important questions about coma patients and their level of awareness. Several staff members who'd witnessed his deliberate choice expressed amazement. I hoped the experience would motivate them to adjust their expectations and guard their speech in the presence of patients who appear unresponsive.

While we were there, we took the opportunity to speak with Dr. Carlile about the possibility of Jacob's returning for intense therapy. We also told her of our desire to bring him home and our hope that a stint at Baylor Rehab might provide a good transition.

She expressed eagerness to treat Jacob again. He had recovered enough to benefit from traditional methods of therapy aimed at developing skills necessary for independent living. Though he still had a long way to go, Jacob had regained enough body control to give the therapists something to work with.

After comparing calendars with Dr. Carlile, we decided Jacob would return to Baylor for seventeen days in March, including the week of my spring break. I would stay in Dallas the entire time, taking an additional week away from my teaching job. This would enable me to be with Jacob every day and participate in his therapy. I also hoped to use the opportunity to seek the staff's advice in making arrangements for Jacob's ongoing needs. We left that day with our plans settled: Jacob would stay at Merritt Plaza until time for his treatment at Baylor, but afterward he would come home!

We drove back to Marshall excited about our plan. Although we dreaded the reaction we expected from Jacob's fans at Merritt Plaza, we chose not to postpone our announcement. When we delivered Jacob back to his room, we proclaimed our news.

The thought of losing Jacob saddened his Merritt Plaza family, but they also realized their successful efforts had made his going home possible. It was a bittersweet victory for Pat and the rest of the staff who had grown to love him. In spite of their impending loss, they plunged in to make the most of their final weeks with Jacob.

Meanwhile, we faced a huge task: preparing our home for Jacob's arrival. Putting him back upstairs was out of the question. George and I agreed Jacob should be as close to our room as possible. The master bedroom in our house is reached by turning left when entering the front foyer, then walking down two steps and through a den. All the other rooms in the house are on the opposite side of the foyer. Given this layout, the den seemed the logical choice for Jacob's new room.

Bill Brock, a professional woodworker from our church, offered to build and donate ramps for our backdoor entrance and the indoor steps to the den. The next step was to transform the room into a place where Jacob's needs could be met and our family and friends could also gather.

One afternoon George stopped by the hospital to visit a friend who'd had surgery. A nurse in the elevator recognized him from our two-week ICU stay. "I remember your family. I think the whole hospital staff remembers how many visitors you had! How is your son doing?"

"Jacob has made remarkable progress. He's still on a feeding tube, but he's walking with assistance. In fact, we're making preparations now to move him home from Merritt Plaza."

She placed her hand on his arm. "That's wonderful! What will you have to do to prepare your home?"

"Mostly we just need to purchase some equipment and line up services. We're also looking for a hospital bed. Since Jacob still receives his food through a stomach tube, we need a hospital bed that can be elevated at the head."

Her face lit up. "We're replacing some of our beds here. They work just fine, but they're older, simpler models, and we're updating. I'll bet the hospital would give you one of the old ones!" She promised to look into it and let us know.

A few days later, a hospital representative called and informed us a bed would be delivered. No charge. At the appointed time, a truck towing a flatbed trailer pulled up in front of our house.

I laughed when I looked out the window and saw a fully made bed, complete with pillow, sheets, and blanket, sitting on the trailer. The two deliverymen came inside, and we discussed the best strategy for getting the bed into the room. Not only did it weigh a ton, manipulating the bed around corners would be difficult, if not impossible.

We finally decided they should carry it around to the backyard, up three steps onto a porch, and in through a door that opens into the den. They were strong and more than willing, but just hauling the bulky load around the house proved exhausting. They heaved and shoved, struggling to negotiate the stairs up to the porch. After several failed attempts, they managed to hoist the bed through the door and then positioned it beside a window at my direction.

The men paused to catch their breath and wipe the sweat from their brows. I offered them glasses of water. While they drank, I asked if they wanted to take the sheets and other bedding back with them.

They smiled, and one of them said, "No, the hospital wants you to have the whole package."

I thanked them, feeling again the insufficiency of words to express our gratitude. After they left, I stood looking at the bed with satisfaction. It bore a few scars from years of use, but to me it symbolized a beautiful promise. Jacob would be coming home soon!

We longed for his arrival, but we also knew some lifestyle changes would accompany him. To help each member of our family handle the adjustment better, we decided to continue participating in most of our usual activities and occupations after Jacob's return. Restructuring our lives to become full-time caregivers would have placed tremendous stress on everyone.

Our insurance would cover the cost of a part-time certified nurse's aide. We asked around, and a local nurse recommended a reputable home health organization. With some trepidation we called, realizing whoever the agency sent would become a significant part of Jacob's life. The aide would also have unlimited access to our home. Having heard and read horror stories about people who take advantage of the disabled, we prayed the right person would be provided. The agency arranged for an aide to begin work upon our return from Baylor.

Through various conversations and inquiries we located equipment suppliers. Before spring break arrived we had recarpeted the room, bought a few new pieces of furniture, and made almost all the necessary arrangements for Jacob's homecoming.

In response to a recommendation we'd brought back from our January visit with Dr. Carlile, the nurses at Merritt Plaza had been tapering off Jacob's medications. By the time he came home, most of them would be discontinued.

During one of my visits with Jacob, Pat Wilson led me to a storage room. "Now, we've tried several brands of food, but this is the one Jacob likes best." She gestured to a stack of cases filled with canned, vanilla-flavored liquid. "You may not think he can taste it, but he can!"

I smiled at her. "I'm sure you're right. We'll keep using that brand."

"I'll give you several cases to take home and a brochure with the ordering information."

I wanted to hug her. I knew how much she loved Jacob—how he inspired her and brightened her days. And yet, Pat was doing everything she could to make the transition smooth. "Thank you, Pat. I wish I could express how much we appreciate you."

She brushed the comment aside. "We all just want the best for Jacob."

I knew I would cry if I continued the conversation. Leaving Merritt Plaza was not going to be easy for anyone involved. We loved them. They had become like family.

On March 3, 1997, we packed Jacob's belongings and transferred them from his room at Merritt Plaza to our house. The items that had been donated by local businesses were considered ours. We took the lamp and dresser, but we left the comforter, curtains, and some other decorative items to make the room homey for the next resident. One by one we said our farewells to the staff and residents.

We walked down those familiar halls for the last time with little fanfare. I looked back, half expecting to see Pat coming to see us off. Everything was quiet. Business as usual in a nursing home. It felt strange, but it also seemed the least painful way to go.

Pam Dowd had offered to come spend the two weeks in Dallas with me and Jacob. I was thrilled to have a friend along for companionship and support. Jacob would be staying at Baylor, but Pam and I would stay at my parents' house.

George drove us to Dallas and helped settle Jacob into his new room. Baylor placed him on the third floor again, but this time he had a private room and didn't require constant observation. The staff gave me a schedule of Jacob's daily therapies. Each morning Pam and I rose early, exercised a little, ate breakfast, and then drove my dad's car downtown to spend the day with Jacob. We returned late in the evening when he was ready for bed. During spring break, George, Grace, Luke, and Natalie joined us.

Some of the members of Jacob's new therapy team had worked with him before. The beefy occupational therapy assistant, T-Bone, once again amused us with his humor while patiently encouraging Jacob to squeeze clothespins or turn oversized screws.

Jacob's occupational therapist, Suzanne, and his speech therapist, Julie, had both been on the original team. They marveled at Jacob's progress since his last stay. With delightful enthusiasm, they worked with Jacob on four main areas: activities of daily living, swallowing, eating, and speech.

These professionals zeroed in on specific skills Jacob needed to develop, and they provided detailed instructions so we could continue helping him improve in the future. Dr. Carlile also encouraged me to use these two intense weeks with Jacob to tackle a major hurdle: toilet training.

Jacob seemed to know when he needed to have a bowel movement, and a panicked expression on his face indicated he disliked using a diaper. At regular intervals throughout the day, I walked him into the private bathroom attached to his room and helped him sit on the toilet. Though he couldn't always make it happen, he knew what he was supposed to do. Jacob began controlling his bowels, waiting for these opportunities to relieve himself.

He often urinated in the toilet as well. His successes excited everyone. As I watched Jacob concentrate on the effort, I could tell he desired to master these skills. Seeing my fifteen-year-old in diapers had been a constant source of sadness. We were all eager to be rid of them, and now liberation looked like a real possibility. Being at Baylor all day enabled me to devote my undivided attention to the project, allowing for significant progress in a short amount of time.

During our two and a half weeks there, staff members provided useful information about a network of other organizations we could contact. I told Dr. Carlile we wanted to find a high-quality therapy center close to home where Jacob could continue to receive professional treatment. She located one with a good reputation.

Dr. Carlile called on our behalf and spoke with the administrator of the Therapy Center in Longview, a town thirty miles from Marshall. Convinced the facility would be suitable for Jacob's ongoing needs, Dr. Carlile made the necessary arrangements for Jacob to be evaluated by their therapists shortly after our return home.

Only one aspect of our second stay at Baylor disappointed me. Perhaps we'd been spoiled by Jacob's former physical therapist, Terri, but the physical therapist assigned to Jacob's team this time didn't seem to have the same energy and spark. And some of the activities she attempted struck me as being unsuited to his current abilities.

One afternoon, she told Jacob to climb a ladder leaning against the therapy room wall. He looked at the ladder and froze. Knowing Jacob, I recognized his strong will had kicked in. Even in my frustration with the therapist's impossible demand, I felt a jolt of excitement when I saw an expression on Jacob's face I'd seen many times before. My son was returning in more ways than one.

We showed up at the soccer field for Jacob's first practice. He was five years old. Jacob looked out the car window at the other kids running around the field kicking balls. He watched for a minute, then leaned back in the seat and refused to get out of the car.

George got out and opened the back door. He ducked his head inside. "Come on, Jacob, let's go. Don't you remember how excited you were about playing soccer?"

"No!"

I turned in the passenger seat and faced Jacob. "But we bought the uniform and the ball . . . you even have your special soccer shoes."

Jacob looked at the shoes, remorse creeping into his expression. He loved those shoes. Then his resolve returned. "I'm not gonna play!"

"Why not?" George and I spoke in unison, our exasperation increasing.

The coach blew his whistle and called the kids to begin practice.

Jacob crossed his arms at his chest. "I don't want to. I wanna go home. I'm not gonna play!" He stared straight ahead, his lips tight.

We decided to confer with the coach, a young surgeon whose son was also on the team. He smiled. "Lots of kids are a little nervous their first time at practice. After he runs around a while and has some fun, he'll forget all about it. Let me talk to him."

George and I waited at a distance from the car. After five or ten minutes, the coach returned, flushed and flustered. He couldn't budge Jacob either. Practice began. After waiting fifteen more minutes, we realized nothing was going to move this three-foot mountain. We drove home.

Although we returned to the field several more times, Jacob never participated in a single practice, let alone a game. After much discussion, we uncovered the truth. He couldn't bring himself to risk failing before an audience.

In later years, Jacob overcame this tendency somewhat, but he always struggled with a desire for perfection. If he didn't think he could do something well, he often wouldn't attempt it at all. I knew Jacob would do anything to avoid guaranteed failure.

I also knew he couldn't climb that ladder.

Perhaps the therapist knew this, too, and was monitoring Jacob's response. At least I could be thankful for one positive outcome from the physical therapy session. Jacob's old personality was emerging.

As our time at Baylor Rehab ended, I realized I'd come there with a degree of misplaced hope. As much as I appreciated all they had done for Jacob, Baylor wasn't a magic place where Jacob could get the perfect combination of therapies to bring about speedy and complete recovery. Such a place didn't exist. The fact that I was disappointed at all indicated I harbored unrealistic expectations.

Jacob had made important progress, but he hadn't been transformed. He still couldn't swallow, eat, or speak. No matter where Jacob went, human beings would remain limited in what they could do for him. We would have to keep our focus on the Lord, Jacob's healer and keeper.

CHAPTER 15

WADING THROUGH NEW WATERS

. . . and [he] led me through the water, water reaching the knees.
—Ezek. 47:4

It's easy to see God's hand at work in retrospect. Looking back at His faithfulness tends to make us wonder why we ever worry. But even when we believe God is able and willing to meet our needs, we still have to walk by faith through present circumstances.

Having a health care professional in our home day after day presented an opportunity to trust God in a brand-new way. We took comfort in knowing we'd hired a reputable agency to screen potential aides, but we couldn't forget horror stories we'd heard about patient abuse or missing valuables.

Jacob would not be able to tell us if his aide mistreated him or did anything else inappropriate. We felt vulnerable and impotent—dependent on the Lord to protect Jacob. As I prayed about those feelings, their irony struck me. In reality we are dependent on God for every breath we take. We just like to think we're in control.

The agency sent Kelly, a certified nurse's aide, to work with Jacob. George and I sized her up as pleasant, sensible, and easygoing—probably in her early twenties. Jacob appeared to be comfortable with her. As we got to know Kelly better, our initial concerns disappeared.

George or I came home each day during the lunch hour, because Kelly's certification didn't authorize her to feed a patient with a feeding tube. In addition to basic physical care, we asked Kelly to provide constant stimulation: talking to Jacob, reading with him, going for walks, and engaging in other activities to promote brain activity. Regular trips to the bathroom furthered Jacob's toilet training progress. While George, Grace, Luke, and I were gone during the day, Kelly stayed at our house with Jacob. We trusted that, in the absence of observers, she would approach her tasks with energy and enthusiasm.

Meanwhile, we still encouraged visitors to come as often as they wished. But as we had predicted, only our close friends felt free to drop by unannounced. We hoped having Jacob home was worth the trade-off. He seemed happy to be there, and he also seemed to be improving. As he regained control of his arms and hands, he sometimes pointed to communicate—another step toward meaningful connection.

By the time we brought Jacob home from Merritt Plaza, we'd already begun to take him on outings around town. One morning I took Jacob to a special chapel service at Trinity school, and I watched him as Philip Jones exalted the power and goodness of God. Jacob listened with an intense expression on his face. At one point, when Philip said "God," Jacob pointed first to his own heart and then straight up in the air.

I gasped at the profound beauty of the gesture. Awe filled me as he repeated the sequence several times, passion burning in his eyes. It was as though he wanted the whole world to know God ruled in his heart and in heaven.

After that day, when someone mentioned the Lord, Jacob pointed. Always to his heart first, then to the sky. He hadn't uttered a single word, but his actions preached a thousand sermons.

Resolved to help Jacob reach his full potential, we prayed for wisdom as we contemplated the many suggestions and leads we received. Multitudes of organizations and therapies exist for brain-injured people, and we had collected stacks of brochures and pamphlets to consider. Some organizations required an extensive long-term commitment to detailed programs; some involved experimental therapies; some seemed a little quackish. We tried not to let our emotions drive us into rash decisions. The temptation to feel guilty about not doing enough always lurked nearby.

After praying for guidance, we ventured forward, trying some therapies for a while, choosing not to try others, trusting God to open the right doors in spite of our ignorance. As difficult as it was to get Jacob on and off an airplane, George and Jacob flew to Utah for an evaluation by one highly recommended organization, the National Academy for Child Development. They prescribed a rigorous program involving aspects of physical, occupational, and speech therapy, cross-patterning, and tactile stimulation. Their philosophy stressed frequency and duration as the keys to successful implementation.

For months we followed the program diligently, which meant hours of effort each day. Some of the exercises required at least two assistants to perform. In the process, we learned many important aspects of brain development and healing. However, maintaining the level of intensity prescribed eventually became too impractical. We remained thankful for the benefits and knowledge gained, and we continued using the concepts and exercises in a more informal manner.

On any given topic, if we asked twenty people, we might receive twenty different opinions. We appreciated helpful advice, but we also realized we couldn't take every fork in the road to recovery. Sometimes we made decisions, then second-guessed them. Again and again we committed our way to the Lord, asking Him to open and close doors to keep us in His will.

In early April, I drove Jacob to Longview for his evaluation at the Therapy Center. After testing his physical and cognitive abilities, they scheduled twice weekly sessions for physical, occupational, and speech therapy. During our first visit, Jacob and I met the therapists who would be working with him. The speech therapist, a spunky young woman named Kristy Stringer, plunged in with enthusiasm. I immediately noticed a difference in her approach.

Donning latex gloves, Kristy asked Jacob to open his mouth so she could press on his teeth with her index finger. As she worked, she explained the reasons behind her methods. "This will help Jacob gain control over his mouth muscles by retraining the brain through external stimulation." She ran her finger along the inside surfaces of Jacob's mouth and used a tongue depressor to press on his tongue.

Kristy told Jacob to move his tongue from side to side, poke it out and push it against the tongue depressor, and curl it over his upper and then lower lip. As I watched Jacob attempting to comply, I realized Kristy's technique made perfect sense. If the brain couldn't send signals to the body, the body could send signals to the brain first to form a reconnection.

Kristy encouraged me to help Jacob practice the exercises at home. The other therapists at the Therapy Center operated under similar philosophies, using methods of outward stimulation to reconnect the body to the brain. In Jacob's case, this proved an effective system. He made noticeable progress from the start.

One might think these encouraging developments would keep me in a positive state of mind. But waves of pain continued to wash over me. As Jacob and I drove down Highway 80 to the Therapy Center, we passed beautiful wildflowers growing in the median. In previous years I'd always loved this stretch of road and admired the brilliant display of color. But now their cheerful beauty seemed to insult my pain.

There were days when tears poured silently down my cheeks as I sped past gorgeous swaths of bright yellow blooms waving in the gentle spring breeze. I often glanced at other drivers in their cars and wondered if any of them were hurting as badly as I was. None of those strangers knew my heart was broken. *Lord, help me be more sensitive to the pain of others. Suffering people are always around me, whether I'm aware of their circumstances or not.*

As Jacob's sixteenth birthday and the first anniversary of his near-drowning approached, I ached remembering how he used to be compared with his current condition. We were truly thankful for every single improvement, believing each was a gift from God. But in many ways, we had lost our son, and deep pain persisted. The Jacob we took care of now was a very different person from the Jacob we had known for fifteen years.

We'd heard pets can produce healing effects in disabled people, so we decided to buy a puppy that spring. Had we wanted a dog solely as a companion for Jacob, we would have opted for an aging golden retriever. However, this dog would serve as a pet for the other children, too, and we wanted something small. We chose a rat terrier and named her Tipper. She was frisky and cute, and all the kids enjoyed her presence. But even as I watched her frolic, sorrowful thoughts intruded. *Tipper's brain works better than Jacob's.* I battled bitterness constantly.

Pam and Natalie Dowd came by to see the new puppy. As I watched Natalie play with Tipper, I imagined her future. She would go off to college, marry, have children, and enjoy life. What did the future hold for Jacob?

Pam noticed the tears in my eyes. "Are you OK?"

"No. Not really."

Pam and I left the kids and Tipper with Jacob and walked through the living room to the kitchen. I filled a carafe with water and poured it into the coffeemaker. "Contemplating the future depresses me."

Pam leaned against the counter. "Your future or Jacob's?"

I scooped coffee into the filter with vengeance, spilling grounds on the counter. "Both. If Jacob stops improving . . . if he remains permanently disabled and dependent on George and me, what happens to the 'golden years' parents are supposed to have together?"

Pam took the washrag from the edge of the sink and brushed the grounds into her hand. She didn't answer.

The voice of self-pity continued in my head. *Children should grow up and move on, building their own lives.* I flipped the switch on the coffeemaker and turned to face Pam. "It's hard for me to look at Natalie and Abigail without feeling jealous. I'm sorry, Pam. I know that probably hurts you. But it's the way I feel. They have so much ahead of them. What does Jacob have to look forward to?"

Pam sighed. "I'm sure it *is* hard for you to see Jacob's friends growing up before your eyes. I wish I could make it easier."

The coffeemaker hissed as dark, steamy liquid dripped into the carafe. Rich aroma permeated the kitchen. "It's very hard. But you want to know the ugly truth? I'm more depressed about what this does to *my* future. The truth is I don't want to spend the rest of my life taking care of Jacob." I stared at a crumb on the floor, then pressed it with my toe. I felt about as low as that crumb. "I imagine God is pretty disgusted with me."

Pam shook her head. "No. God is *not* disgusted. He understands you. He sees your fears, and He's patient and merciful. God will give you the strength and resources you need for whatever lies ahead."

I poured coffee into two mugs and stirred in French vanilla creamer. "Yeah. I know all the right Bible verses. I should 'not be anxious about tomorrow'; instead I should pray . . . and 'I can do all things through Christ.' I *do* believe God holds the future in His hands. What I can't seem to believe is that I'm going to like it!"

Pam smiled and reached for a mug. "I don't have to tell you what to do. You already know. And I know you believe God is faithful to His promises."

I sipped my coffee. "I do believe. And I'm thankful for all God has already done. I truly am. The challenge right now is to keep coming to Him for grace and power to live minute by minute. If I can figure out how to do that, maybe I'll find joy in living each day with the Lord."

"There's no 'maybe' about it. The future holds more opportunities to see God accomplish His purposes. Don't listen to self-pity."

Don't listen? That's easier said than done. I watched the steam rising from my cup. "Pray for me, Pam. Self-pity still shows up almost every day. Pray I'll have the strength to slam the door in its ugly face."

Pam hugged me. "I am praying for you. All the time and with all my heart."

People continued to come forward offering to help in many ways. George's cousin, Roxanne, and her husband, Trapper, lived in Seattle. He'd retired from a position at Microsoft and contacted us expressing his and Roxanne's desire to provide software for Jacob. As Jacob gained greater control of his hands, the computer could become a valuable aid to his ongoing progress. We accepted Trapper's offer and tried to establish some guidelines to help him choose appropriate games and programs.

Before long, a package arrived in the mail containing a wonderful variety of games and activities, ranging from simple math tutorials to clay-mation adventures. Trapper proved thoughtful and creative in his selections, and the generous quantity they sent overwhelmed us. Grace and Luke were particularly excited about this donation, because it would mean hours of fun entertainment for them, too.

Each person who reached out to Jacob and our family offered gifts in keeping with a unique knowledge or ability. The combination of individuals and their expertise provided a rich environment of stimulation and support, leaving us with a sense of amazement and humble gratitude. Every contribution—great or small—made a difference.

For physical exercise, we escorted Jacob through the neighborhood. Though his balance remained tentative, he required less and less assistance, managing alone on flat, even surfaces. Sometimes we lifted him onto the trampoline in our backyard. George climbed on with him and helped him stand. Then, holding both of Jacob's hands in his, George gently bounced. Jacob loved it when his feet left the trampoline bed and he was momentarily airborne. His face broke into a huge grin, and he laughed with abandon.

One afternoon several of us stood beside the trampoline watching them jump, enjoying the welcome sound of Jacob's laughter. When George and Jacob stopped for a short break, Amy Barron, a college student who was living with us at the time, said, "Jacob, if you want to jump some more, say 'Mom.'"

"Mom."

We all froze. The word had been clear and unmistakable. As soon as Jacob said it, a startled expression came over his face. Then he smiled, looking self-conscious and shy.

Amy began to cry. I could hardly believe what I had just heard. George hugged Jacob and encouraged him to say it again, but the moment had passed. It was as though Jacob had reacted without thinking. Now that he wanted to speak, he couldn't figure out how. We didn't mind, though. We knew the potential was there!

<hr />

Music had continued to make Jacob cry for a couple of months after the first time it happened at Merritt Plaza. Then he seemed to gain control over the tendency. But one song still produced a profound effect. Jacob loved the movie "Toy Story." We owned the video, and he was eager to watch it whenever we let him. At one point in the movie Buzz Lightyear comes to grips with the fact that he is only a toy, not a real space ranger. During the scene, a song is playing on the soundtrack. The lyrics tell the story of Buzz's emerging comprehension of his limitations, ending with the line, "I will go sailing no more."

As the song is coming to a close, Buzz attempts to fly off a second-story landing and out a window, but he falls in slow motion to the steps below, breaking into several pieces, a look of sad reconciliation on his face. Though Jacob usually made it through the first part of the scene without crying, by the end he would be sobbing in apparent sympathy for the broken toy. If we hadn't believed the sense of identification and the emotional response were cathartic for Jacob, we would have spared him and ourselves the experience. It wasn't easy to listen to those words and watch him weep.

Even though the school year was drawing to a close, we wanted to check into the possibility of enrolling Jacob in a program at the local high school. His therapists at the Therapy Center believed Jacob would benefit from interaction with his peers. Once again, we entered new territory. Grace and Luke still attended the accelerated classes at Trinity, and Jacob's past experience had been in that same environment. We were about to be introduced to the world of special education.

The first classroom George, Jacob, and I visited served students with severe physical and mental disabilities. Though the teacher was kind and solicitous, we found ourselves surrounded by an atmosphere of general chaos. Jacob sat in a chair, a sober look on his face. Students ranging in age from five years old to about seventeen called to the teacher from wheelchairs or made unintelligible sounds. There were several aides in the room, but they all seemed to have their hands quite full.

George and I felt the same way we had after our visit to the children's facility in Gladewater. It was impossible. We couldn't bring Jacob into this place. We wanted him to be surrounded by his peers in an environment similar to his former one. This classroom offered nothing familiar. We thanked the teacher, but knew we'd have to find something else.

Next Jacob and I visited a special ed classroom at the high school. Taught by a gentle, soft-spoken man named Mr. King, this class contained students between the ages of fifteen and twenty-one. They sat at desks, performing simple tasks. Some completed uncomplicated building projects. Others worked on written assignments. The students were mostly well behaved and respectful. I could see they liked their teacher.

Jacob was not as functional as these students, but Kelly, his aide, would be there to help him if he joined the class. I had to swallow my pride and refuse to dwell on the vast differences between Jacob's former status as an honor student and his prospects in this setting. Having seen the other option, Mr. King's realm looked promising.

Jacob and I attended an initial Admission, Review and Dismissal (ARD) Committee meeting and developed an Individual Education Plan (IEP) Report on April 23, 1997. These meetings are a cornerstone in the world of special education. After evaluation, the committee placed Jacob in Mr. King's class for the remainder of the school year. Kelly would accompany him to school. He would also receive physical, occupational, and speech therapy through the school therapists, in addition to his sessions at the Therapy Center in Longview. In the fall, another ARD would be scheduled to determine any progress made over the summer and to formulate a new plan.

◆◆◇◆◆

Each time we waded into new waters—in-home health care, new therapists, school—I longed to see dramatic results. In today's world, so many of life's conveniences are instantaneous. The last thing I wanted to do was wait. I believed God's promises, but I wanted answers right away. Yet during the months following Jacob's return home, I encountered many opportunities to practice patience.

One late-spring evening I sat outside enjoying a pleasant breeze and fiery sunset. I'd been reading Genesis the past few days, and I thought about how God promised Abraham a son. Isaac was born twenty-five years later. During those years, God prepared Abraham to be the father of the nation Israel. Much of Abraham's preparation involved the strengthening of his faith. "Abraham believed God, and it was counted to him as righteousness." God didn't cut corners with Abraham, because God had planned for the Messiah of all nations to come through Israel.

Lord, I realize You desire faith. If I believe You in the process, the results become secondary. Your purposes have already been accomplished. Help me trust You as Abraham did, even when the promises seem impossible.

I watched the last embers of sunset flicker and die, and I stood to go inside. A star winked in the eastern sky. *Can you count the stars, Abraham?* Peace settled over me with the deep blue blanket of night. If I could trust God without knowing how much Jacob would recover, the victory would already be won in God's sight. Faith perfected, and Christ honored.

I resolved to let God carry me through my days, one by one. His mercies are new every morning, and I wanted to be aware of them. Blessings can turn up where we least expect them. For example, one day the phone rings, and the person on the other end of the line is an angel in disguise. An angel in cowboy boots.

CHAPTER 16

RIPPLES REVEAL HEROES

Blessed be the God and Father of our Lord Jesus Christ, the Father of mercies and God of all comfort; who comforts us in all our affliction so that we will be able to comfort those who are in any affliction with the comfort with which we ourselves are comforted by God.

—2 Cor. 1:3–4

Living in East Texas, we're accustomed to thick accents. But when the phone rang one day in May, the voice behind the twang sounded unfamiliar.

"Hi, Mrs. Damoff? This is Ronnie Foster. I've been followin' all the articles in the paper about your son, and I was just callin' to see if you'd be interested in horseback ridin' for Jacob. I have horses, and I could take him. I wouldn't charge you anything."

"Horseback riding? Wow, Ronnie, thanks. It's so great of you to offer. But I'm not sure Jacob could do it. He's not strong. . . . How would he even get on the horse? He's just recently started walking unassisted, and someone is always right there with him. His balance isn't good. I'd be afraid he might fall off."

"I understand your concerns, ma'am, but I think it would be worth a try. It sure helped me. I've had several strokes, and after every one I got back on my horses as soon as I could. It always helped me recover much faster. I'm not a trained therapist or anything, but I'm a firm believer in it."

"Let me talk to my husband, George. Then he'll call you back. OK?"

George and I had heard of therapy using horses, or "hippotherapy." In our search for brain-injury treatments, we'd read articles about how it had gained popularity in recent years. People suffering from a wide range of physical and emotional disabilities experienced dramatic, often unexpected improvement. Theory states that the rhythm of the horse's movements produces a positive reaction in the brain and body.

We decided to give it a try. When we met Ronnie at the gate to the pasture, he looked like a movie cowboy minus the hat and six-shooter. Wiry, strong, and sun-tanned, he had chiseled facial features, thick gray hair, and sparkling blue eyes. We soon discovered he was as demanding as he was kind.

The horse—a large, gray appaloosa named Pretty Boy—appeared calm as he grazed nearby. Ronnie entered the pasture with the horse's tack and saddle. Pretty Boy cooperated with the saddling, which I took to be a good sign of his temperament and his affection for Ronnie.

After some discussion about the best way to get Jacob on the horse, Ronnie and George hoisted him into the saddle. Jacob tensed and his eyes grew wide. His mouth contorted in a frightened grimace.

Ignoring Jacob's reaction, Ronnie adjusted Jacob's feet in the stirrups and placed the reins in his hand. Then, with George striding alongside, Ronnie led Pretty Boy around the pasture.

Almost every afternoon they repeated the routine. George returned home from work, took Jacob to meet Ronnie, and for an hour or two they plodded around the pasture. Sometimes George rode behind Jacob. Other days Natalie, Grace, or I tagged along to ride with Jacob.

Ronnie talked to Jacob the whole time, gently prodding him with his wry comments and humor. "Jacob, hold on to those reins! And sit up straight. I swear you ride like a drunken cowboy. I said sit up! You're so stubborn, your head must be full of cement." As harsh as his words sounded, every one had a smile behind it.

Jacob laughed at the remarks. He remained a little hesitant and uncertain about the horse, but he always listened to Ronnie and tried to comply with his demands.

We saw almost instantaneous results. On horseback, Jacob's posture improved, and his flexed wrists relaxed. We also noticed that whenever he was riding, he swallowed. We never once had to offer him a towel for spitting out his saliva, and his shirtfront remained dry. Kristy's activities at the Therapy Center had enhanced his swallowing ability, but he only swallowed with perfect consistency while riding Pretty Boy.

"I believe it's the fear of fallin' that keeps a rider on a horse," Ronnie explained to George and me. "As the horse moves, the rider has to adjust his balance to stay on. The brain *and* the muscles get a good workout."

Jacob's legs grew visibly stronger, and Ronnie pushed him harder as the days passed. Though Jacob sometimes looked frightened when riding, a big grin spread across his face whenever he saw Ronnie.

After only three weeks of hippotherapy, Jacob was swallowing well enough to begin eating. Not too much later, he began making sounds. He produced mostly unintelligible grunts, but he was vocalizing. The first day Jacob spoke while riding, Ronnie admitted he went home and cried.

Determined to push the limits, Ronnie started making Jacob help saddle the horse. When I watched, I had to bite my tongue. On uneven surfaces Jacob often fell. And when Jacob fell, he landed like an axed tree. He never caught himself or displayed normal protective reflexes. As Jacob staggered under the saddle's weight, I braced myself for a catastrophe.

Ronnie stood by to assist, but he wouldn't step in until Jacob's muscles trembled from the effort. If Jacob looked like he was about to quit, Ronnie pushed even more. It amazed me to see how hard Jacob tried when Ronnie instructed him. But Ronnie responded with comments like "Jacob, I told you to bring the saddle over to the gate. I swear your head must be a block of wood." Jacob just laughed and tried harder. He seemed to love Ronnie's insults as much as he loved Ronnie.

At the end of the ride, Jacob had to help unsaddle the horse and reload the gear into Ronnie's truck. No matter how much he stumbled around, Ronnie remained relentless. George and I both cringed. More than once Jacob stumbled, fell, and suffered minor bumps and scrapes.

But we didn't dare interfere with Ronnie! As hard as it was to watch, we believed Ronnie's therapy was exactly what Jacob needed.

Seven weeks after Ronnie began working with Jacob, the *Marshall News Messenger* sent a staff writer to photograph their session and write a story about Ronnie for an installment in a weekly feature called "Everyday Heroes." The article appeared on June 23, 1997. We loved the story and picture of Jacob smiling down at Ronnie from his perch in the saddle. But we would have given the feature a different name. Ronnie was much more than an "everyday hero" to us.

It would be impossible to determine how much good Ronnie accomplished in the hours he spent with Jacob. As for Ronnie, he took little credit for the amazing progress Jacob made. The credit, he said, belonged to God.

That summer, with the help of Ronnie and the Therapy Center, Jacob crossed some major hurdles. As he mastered swallowing, we gradually introduced a variety of foods into his diet without any evidence of problems. We were thrilled when the doctor agreed it was time to remove the feeding tube from Jacob's stomach.

After a year on a liquid, tube-fed diet, Jacob could once again enjoy the wonderful flavors and textures of real food! Tasting and chewing also served to provide additional stimulation to Jacob's mouth, enhancing his speech capabilities.

George and I are both musicians, and Jacob possessed a beautiful soprano voice as a child. Before his second birthday, he'd memorized the songs and hymns we sang to him. If we omitted the final word in a line, Jacob warbled it in clear, sweet baby tones.

At some point during the summer of 1997, our family drove to Dallas for a visit with my parents. On the return trip, we made a remarkable discovery. As George, Grace, Luke, and I sang along with the radio, we heard Jacob trying to participate. We turned off the music and began singing songs Jacob had known before his accident, leaving off the last word of each line. Just as he had done as a baby, Jacob attempted to fill in the missing words. Though he usually managed to aspirate only the initial sound of the word, his intentions were unmistakable.

As much as his efforts to speak amazed us, we were even more overwhelmed by his memory. From the sounds he made, we could tell he knew the last word to every line of every song we sang, from "Mary Had a Little Lamb" to selections from CDs he'd received as gifts on his birthday two weeks before the accident. We drove home that day in a state of pure bliss, singing song after song, never ceasing to marvel as he recalled them all.

As we passed through Longview on our way to Marshall, we noticed the youth bus had just returned to Natalie's church from summer camp. We pulled into the parking lot and found her there surrounded by her friends. Surprised to see us, she ran up to the van and opened the side door beside Jacob's seat. We turned to him and said, "Jacob, who is that?"

Natalie scanned our faces to see if we were serious. Then she looked back at Jacob, but he turned his face away. His shy expression made us wonder if he realized he couldn't make the sounds as clearly as he wished. The Jacob we had known before would be hesitant to try if he thought he might fail.

Natalie waited, whispering encouragement for Jacob to say her name. Finally, still looking down, he muttered, "Na-ta . . . Jay . . . Dow . . ." Natalie Jane Dowd.

She squealed with delight and threw her arms around him in a big hug. Natalie turned a face full of eager hope back toward us. "This is it, isn't it?"

We had all waited for a long time to hear Jacob's voice. For a year, we had been unable to find any reliable method by which Jacob could communicate. Vast horizons opened before us now. Meeting Natalie in the parking lot seemed the perfect conclusion to an amazing afternoon. Jacob was regaining speech, and he was revealing a storehouse of memories. We couldn't wait to find out what else he had to say.

As speech returned, we began to get to know Jacob again in earnest and discovered some major memory deficits. Math was gone. He remembered numbers, could count, and could even count by fives or tens with prompting. But he couldn't add two plus two. With tutoring, Jacob made small progress, but he still couldn't seem to grasp and retain mathematical concepts.

Jacob's vocabulary, on the other hand, amazed us from the start. He struggled with articulation, as though a dentist had numbed his whole mouth, but the words and their meanings were all there. We marveled at the way certain situations stimulated language memory, causing Jacob to blurt out a sophisticated phrase or concept perfectly suited to the circumstances.

For example, Jacob loved watching slapstick comedy, so we bought videos of the Peter Sellers "Pink Panther" movies. In one opening scene, a thief steals a diamond necklace from a safe and replaces it with his calling card, a monogrammed glove. We'd all settled in to enjoy the show one evening when, from his cushiony recliner, Jacob astounded us by saying, "Jewel heist."

We looked at him in wonder. "That's right, Jacob," I agreed. "It's a jewel heist. That's not a very common phrase, though. Why do you suppose you thought of it?"

"I don't know."

Neither did we. The more Jacob said, the more I wished I could get inside his brain to understand its workings.

Because Jacob slurred his speech, people who didn't know him tended to underestimate the depth of his verbal comprehension. In group settings, he listened and could follow almost any conversation, no matter how advanced the subject matter. Often, when a speaker paused to reflect or search for the right word, Jacob spoke up and supplied it, startling everyone.

What to do with a five-thousand-dollar, state-of-the-art, tilt-in-space wheelchair with "Jacob" monogrammed on the seat-back in gold block letters?

The Cadillac of a wheelchair custom-designed for Jacob by the Baylor Rehab therapists had been slow in coming. The first time the company sent it, a problem with the frame forced us to return the chair to the manufacturer for reconstruction. Almost the whole duration of Jacob's stay at Merritt Plaza, he'd used an inexpensive, collapsible chair owned by the nursing home. By the time we finally received the fancy chair, we had little use for it. Jacob was walking.

We hadn't had the chair long when the phone rang one afternoon. The caller identified herself as Joanna Blackwelder. In her sweet, quiet voice she explained that someone who knew about our son had given her our name and phone number. Perhaps we might be able to offer suggestions or encouragement in her family's present situation.

I listened as she unfolded the story of her ten-year-old son's drowning accident in May, almost exactly one year after Jacob's. Now, a couple of months later, he remained semicomatose in a hospital in Ruston, Louisiana. They were anxiously watching for any signs of recovery.

It broke my heart to imagine them in the same circumstances we had faced a year earlier. I was thankful I could share with her about the significant progress we'd seen. No one had been available to offer me the same hope when I was in her shoes.

Joanna wanted to know if we had other children and, if so, how they were handling the ordeal. I began to explain, "Our son who nearly drowned is named Jacob. He is the oldest, but we also have a daughter, Grace, and our youngest is named Luke—"

"Your son's name is Jacob?" she interrupted.

"Yes, that's right."

"My son is the oldest child, also, and he has a younger sister, Casey, and a brother named Cody. But, Jeanne, you won't believe this! My older son's name is Jacob. We call him Jake."

We were both struck by the similarities between our families. As the conversation progressed, we shared more openly about our beliefs. It became obvious that Joanna possessed a genuine faith in Christ. I promised to pray for them and to keep in touch. Then I had an idea.

"Joanna, we have a wheelchair. It's a custom-made model designed for Jacob by physical therapists, with all kinds of special support features beneficial to someone in coma. It's worth five thousand dollars, but it didn't cost us anything. Insurance covered it. Jacob doesn't need it, and we'd be so happy if we knew it was being put to good use. Would you like to have it?"

"It sounds wonderful! We'd love to have it, if you're sure you're ready to give it up."

"I can honestly say we are eager to. Oh, and it even has the name 'Jacob' monogrammed on the back of the seat."

"Are you serious? This is so amazing!"

I felt more thankful than ever for the healing in Jacob's life, liberating him first from the trach, then the feeding tube, and now the wheelchair. As happy as meeting Jake's need made me feel, I hoped the Blackwelders wouldn't need the chair for long.

We had already planned a trip to Florida, and our route would take us not far from Ruston. We arranged to visit the Blackwelders in the hospital and drop off the wheelchair. As we entered the lobby, we saw a tall, beautiful woman, probably in her early thirties, with long blonde hair and a genuine smile. Joanna smiled and greeted us. Her gentle eyes expressed sorrow mixed with peace. She took us to the room where Jake and the rest of her family were waiting.

Joanna introduced us to her physician husband, Mark, in the hall. Entering the room, we noticed Jake shared his father's dark coloring, but Casey and Cody were fair and blond like their mother.

The younger children's faces lit up at the sight of Grace and Luke. They scrambled around the back of their brother's bed, chattering their excitement.

Luke grinned, and I caught a look of patient indulgence and amusement in Grace's eyes as the energetic youngsters led her and Luke out into the hall.

George, Jacob, and I approached the bed with Joanna. At the sight of Jake's vacant expression, my mind filled with vivid memories of standing beside Jacob's hospital bed, wondering if he would ever come back to us. But now Jacob stood with us beside someone else's bed.

I watched Jacob as he looked at Jake with a calm, steady gaze. "Jacob, this is Jake, and he almost drowned."

"Just like me." The words slurred like a vinyl record set on a too slow speed.

"Yes, and his family is praying he'll improve just like you. We need to pray for Jake, OK?"

"Yeah."

"And we're also giving him your wheelchair, because you don't need it anymore."

"Yeah. I can walk now." Jacob looked at Joanna and Mark, a peaceful smile spreading across his face.

Joanna's eyes filled with tears. She slipped her arm through mine. "Seeing Jacob is so encouraging for us. Thank you for coming here . . . for the wheelchair, and for this wonderful hope you've brought us."

We stayed and talked with Joanna and Mark for about half an hour. As we prepared to leave, Casey and Cody begged Grace and Luke not to go. The whole family said Luke's gregarious manner and quick wit reminded them of Jake's best friend. We would have lingered, but we had many miles of highway to cover that day.

Before we left the lobby, Joanna gave Jacob a Louisiana State University T-shirt they'd bought as a thank-you gift. When George turned our van out of the parking lot, I glanced at the hospital entrance. Joanna's children stood beside her, waving. We opened the windows and waved back until we pulled out of sight.

As we continued our journey toward Florida, I thought about the joy Jacob had brought to the Blackwelder family. Throughout the course of the past year, many heroes had come into our lives. For the Blackwelders, Jacob was a hero.

The first time Jacob spoke my name on the trampoline, I treasured the simple utterance like a sweet foretaste of good things to come. Many glorious advances graced our days that summer. Before it was over, God gave me another precious gift.

One day I found Jacob standing at the foot of the stairs staring up at his bedroom door. "What are you doing, Jacob?"

"My old room." Jacob concentrated to articulate the molasses-thick words.

"Would you like to go up there?"

"Yeah."

With George moving up the steps in front, holding both of Jacob's arms, and me behind, supporting his back, we helped Jacob climb the stairs for the first time. He sat on the bed and looked around the room in silence. Much still remained as he had left it.

Suddenly joy flooded my heart as I remembered the day I'd come up-stairs to clean. When I'd broken down sobbing, the Lord had spoken.

"Jacob will come back to this room."

Jacob now sat in the same spot where I had collapsed in sorrow that day. I looked at the hand-lettered sign still posted above his door. Yes, Jacob. Today is the greatest day, and you are in it.

CHAPTER 17

CRESTS AND VALLEYS

The one who doubts is like the surf of the sea, driven and tossed by the wind.

—Jas. 1:6

In August, one year and three months after the accident, we received a phone call from Trinity Episcopal Church's insurance company. The caller wanted to schedule a meeting to "settle Jacob's claim." We weren't sure what he meant. We'd made it clear from the beginning we had no intention of suing the church or pressing charges of any kind against anyone involved in the drowning incident.

We decided to call Sam Moseley, a lawyer we knew, to ask his opinion. He agreed to go along with us to the meeting, in case we needed advice. Assembled on one side of the conference table were Philip Jones (Trinity's rector, who had pulled Jacob out of the water), the church's attorney, and the insurance company representative. George and I sat on the other side with Sam Moseley and Mark McMahon, a personal injury attorney Sam invited for consultation. We waited for someone to speak.

Philip broke the silence. "Trinity wishes to accept responsibility for Jacob's accident." He smiled and looked at George, then me. "We initiated this meeting to begin the necessary process to release funds from our insurance company. The church wants to provide for Jacob's current and future financial needs."

The insurance representative then stated the amount of money available in the policy. "If you believe that amount is insufficient for Jacob's needs, you will have to sue the church for an additional settlement."

"We've never had any desire to sue the church," I assured them. I glanced at George sitting beside me. He looked as shocked as I felt. What was actually happening here began to sink in. "I'm sure the amount you quoted is more than adequate."

The church's attorney spoke next. "In order to release the money from the insurance policy, a 'friendly' lawsuit must be filed. It's a necessary formality. No one intends to contest the claims the lawsuit will propose."

Philip may have sensed our unspoken concern. "Don't worry. This action will place no financial burden on the church or harm its assets in any way." He seemed to be suppressing a desire to shout, Hallelujah! "I hope you'll accept the church's offer and file the suit."

Mark McMahon grinned at us and shook his head. "You won't be needing my assistance." He stood and shook Sam Moseley's hand as he excused himself from the meeting.

Sam looked stunned. None of us had anticipated such a generous, unsolicited offer. I scanned the faces on the opposite side of the table. The insurance representative smiled weakly, but Philip beamed at us with radiant joy in his eyes. Before he'd entered seminary, Philip had practiced law with a prominent firm in Waco, Texas. More than anyone else present, he understood the full scope of the meeting's significance.

George and I stared at each other, shook our heads in speechless amazement, and then turned to Sam. "OK," George said. "Go ahead and make the necessary arrangements."

George and I left the meeting in a daze. God had been blessing us in astounding ways with Jacob's recent improvement. As Ephesians 3:20 (NKJV) states, we'd already seen God "do exceeding abundantly beyond all that we ask or think." This new development, however, had never entered our wildest dreams.

For the past year we'd been thankful for a good insurance policy and the generosity of many caring friends and relatives. We tried not to worry about the future. But if Jacob remained dependent and outlived

George and me, we feared he would become a financial burden to his siblings. It had been a constant matter of prayer.

The money the church intended to supply, if placed in a trust fund and wisely invested, would be enough to take care of Jacob for the rest of his life. Still in shock at the idea of such an unbelievable possibility, we prayed all would go according to God's plan.

Before our scheduled court appearance, the judge assigned attorney Brad Morin to represent Jacob's interests in the case. Brad came by our house to meet Jacob. He was friendly and considerate, but he explained part of his job was to prevent George and me from taking for ourselves what was intended for Jacob. We understood the serious nature of his role, but it struck us as humorous. The last thing we wanted to do was rob Jacob.

George and I met with Bob Smith, a financial advisor with Edward Jones Company, to discuss setting up a trust for Jacob if the case went as expected. The insurance company wanted to pay the settlement in yearly installments, but Bob recommended taking a lump sum and investing it ourselves.

When our court date arrived, George and I met Sam Moseley and Bob Smith at the courthouse. We filed into the second row and sat behind Brad Morin. I spotted the church's attorney and insurance representative sitting on the opposite side of the courtroom. Before Judge Bonnie Leggat entered, Brad turned and greeted us. Then he leaned toward me and whispered, "Judge Leggat has a reputation for favoring the interests of children. She will most likely want to direct the handling of any awarded funds."

"OK," I said, smiling. Didn't he know I also favored Jacob's interests? Perhaps he recognized Bob Smith and wondered what arrangements we had made with him.

The court session opened, and the bailiff called me to the stand. Trinity's attorney questioned me about events on the day of the accident. Then he asked, "What were you told regarding Jacob's chances for recovery by the medical professionals at Baylor?"

"They didn't think he had any chance. At one point they even said it would be ethical to remove the feeding tube and let him die." The memory still made me shudder. "They didn't expect Jacob to recover. But we never gave up hope."

George later told me he thought the judge had tears in her eyes during my testimony. She's a judge, but she's also a mother.

The attorney asked questions about our future expectations and Jacob's ongoing needs. Brad Morin spoke up from his seat on the front row. "Will you need to purchase a van?"

"We already have a van."

"But will you need one with specialized features," he pressed, "if Jacob recovers enough to begin to drive?"

"Oh, that would be wonderful! Yes, in that case, I guess we might. But we have a van my parents bought after Jacob's accident. It works fine for our current situation."

Brad looked a little embarrassed. Perhaps he felt, as I did, the irony of our exchange. Unlike most court cases, every attorney on both sides of the courtroom seemed eager to see us win.

I realized my testimony would have to justify our receiving Trinity's generous settlement offer, but I had no intention of painting an overly gloomy picture of the future just to gain the court's sympathy. I kept my answers short and honest. I also expressed our hope that Jacob would continue to make progress in his recovery as he had in recent months.

The bailiff dismissed me to my seat and Judge Leggat called the attorneys to approach the bench. The judge awarded the full settlement. As they closed out the case, the attorneys asked her how the money should be distributed. She responded, "Do whatever the Damoffs tell you to do. They are going to take care of that boy."

Judge Leggat's comment caught me as off guard as it did the attorneys. They turned their surprised faces toward us. Bob Smith had brought a printout of the plan we'd discussed. We showed it to the attorneys, explaining that a large amount would be placed in a trust fund for Jacob. We would be free to invest the rest in anticipation of future needs, such as our other children's college expenses. The court approved our plan.

Afterward, Brad stopped me in the hall. "I've never heard her say anything like that before." He looked dumbfounded but also happy.

"Everyone in the courthouse is talking about it. You people must be very special."

I smiled, still too numb and amazed to know how to respond. Had this happened because we were special? I knew myself too well to think so. It was mercy.

God poured out financial blessings we didn't seek or expect, filling us with a sense of awe we've never lost. We had prayed for provision, and we'd been humbled and blessed by the sacrificial gifts of friends and family. This new development went beyond imagination.

People dream of winning the lottery or of coming into instant money by some unexpected means. They envision the nice house or fancy car they would buy, or the exotic vacations they would take. Gaining wealth had never been one of our priorities. Compared to most of the world, we already lived in luxury. As long as we could afford to pay our bills and stay out of debt, we remained content.

This sudden change in our financial landscape produced amazement and gratitude, but fear crept in as well. We'd heard stories about the destructive effects large sums of money can have on marriages and families. Determined not to fall into those traps, we laid it all before the Lord and prayed for wisdom.

George and I both desired to honor the Lord in these matters, and that unity spared us from much heartache and conflict. Neither of us wanted to change our lifestyle, and yet we welcomed a little financial breathing room. The settlement funds enabled us to repay my parents for the van they had purchased. Though we knew they wouldn't have demanded reimbursement, we loved being able to do it.

We'd been on the receiving end of much generosity. The thought that we could now offer some in return blessed us. As long as we viewed ourselves as stewards of God's property and remembered our accountability to Him, we believed He would lead us in our financial choices.

With Jacob's needs covered, we decided we should close the local account set up for contributions. I wrote letters expressing our deep gratitude to those who had made deposits in the account. I explained that, as much as we valued their love for Jacob and our family, their thoughtful generosity had met a need that no longer existed. We wanted to free them to direct their resources toward others.

For years I had loved patterning my personal prayers after the phrases in the Lord's Prayer. When I came to the part about asking for our daily bread, I thought not only of food and material provision, but of all I needed in a given day: wisdom, guidance, discipline, and conviction of sin.

In the financial realm, the insurance settlement looked like a truck-load of daily bread. I gladly acknowledged God's hand at work in that amazing event, but I still found myself slow to recognize the benefits when God chose to provide me with difficulties to overcome. Even with the miraculous blessings we'd received, I encountered frequent obstacles to victorious faith in God. Each new development in Jacob's condition or schedule included its own set of questions and decisions.

George and I had been relieved at how well everyone in the family had adjusted to having a certified nurse's aide in our home. Kelly had settled into a pleasant, workable routine. However, a few months after she began working with Jacob, the home health organization offered Kelly a position in their office. The agency sent a second aide to observe Kelly in preparation to take her place working with Jacob.

From the start, Jacob didn't like the new aide. His speech and strength of will had both improved enough to make his opinions unmistakable. The problems were personal, not professional, and we fretted over what to do. The agency possessed full control over whom they chose to send, and the aide performed her duties as well as could be expected under the circumstances. Jacob's uncooperative, belligerent attitude didn't help.

Her entrance into the room was enough to set him off. She'd sit on the couch, and he'd get up and leave as fast as his awkward gait allowed. When she rose to follow, he'd slam a door in her face.

We prayed for direction as the uncomfortable months passed. Meanwhile, Jacob resisted all her attempts to encourage his progress, and we grieved the loss of precious time and potential improvement.

The experts at Baylor Rehab had said there is usually about a three-year window of opportunity for recovery with brain injury. Then it would most likely stop. If Jacob refused to work with his aide, progress would slow or cease altogether.

Should we call the home health organization and insist they remove this aide? What if the next one proved to be no better, or even worse? From what we had been told, keeping good nurse's aides on staff is an ongoing challenge for home health agencies. We had asked God to provide the right person. Were we supposed to assume our dilemma was His will? We didn't know the answers.

After a few months, the agency sent an additional aide, a sweet older woman named Priscilla, who only desired to work part-time. The two aides alternated days, and Jacob's behavior extremes reflected an obvious preference for Priscilla. School had started, and the aide on duty accompanied Jacob, taking him to his classes and guiding him through his assigned tasks. He cooperated with Priscilla at school, but even there he tried to escape from the other aide. Our frustration grew.

We considered our options. I could quit my teaching job and become Jacob's full-time attendant. For the sake of my own health and sanity, I didn't think this would be a wise decision. Getting away from home and setting my mind on other matters for a while each day reenergized me to face the emotional and physical stresses associated with Jacob's injury.

We could look into a different agency but with no guarantee of better results. Or we could endure, not knowing how it would all be resolved, but trusting God to work it out and to accomplish His good purposes. We chose to leave things as they were and wait for God's clear guidance. The following spring He brought us a gift worth waiting for.

One afternoon I returned home to find Jacob sitting in the den with the snubbed aide and a new trainee. Always interested in anyone who would be working with Jacob, I took mental notes of my first impressions. Rusty Mauldin, a young man in his early twenties, wasn't much taller than my five-foot-three inches, wore wire-rimmed glasses, and had sandy-colored hair and a mustache. When I introduced myself, he responded in a soft-spoken, polite manner.

I watched Rusty interact with Jacob. Having a male aide around the house would be different for all of us. The question was, would it be better or worse? I might not feel free to walk around in my pajamas, but if Jacob liked Rusty . . .

Jacob laughed at something Rusty said, and the beautiful smile on Jacob's face told me this could be very good.

For a while, Rusty worked part-time along with the two female aides. Then, to everyone's relief, the agency began dividing Jacob's schedule between Priscilla and Rusty. When Priscilla decided to pursue a different occupation, Rusty became Jacob's sole aide.

We couldn't have been more pleased. We all loved Priscilla, but she was like a grandmother figure. Jacob accepted Rusty as a peer. And Rusty seemed to have the perfect personality for the job. He knew when to push Jacob and when to give him space. No matter how obstinate Jacob became, I never saw Rusty lose his patience.

As we got to know Rusty, we learned that he and his wife, Amanda, had married while still in their teens. Having been raised in the country, Rusty possessed strong family values and an honest work ethic. He loved his wife and baby daughter, Nikki, and as time passed, he grew to love Jacob as well. Though Rusty came to us as an aide, he became a true friend. Jacob knew it and loved him.

Rusty brought out the best in Jacob. When he worked with Rusty, Jacob's former dry sense of humor resurfaced with a softer edge. One pleasant afternoon, Jacob and Rusty were bouncing on our backyard trampoline. After fifteen minutes or so, Rusty said, "Jacob, I guess it's about time we crawl off."

As if on cue, the trampoline bed ripped in half, and Jacob and Rusty found themselves sprawled on the ground. Concerned that Jacob might be hurt, Rusty scrambled to his feet to check Jacob for injuries. "Are you OK?"

Jacob looked up at him and replied in a matter-of-fact tone. "I guess we won't have to crawl off."

George and I laughed when Rusty related the story, thrilled at the evidence of Jacob's old personality returning. We also rejoiced over Rusty. We'd found our dream aide. The situation almost seemed too good to be true.

As it turned out, it almost was.

CHAPTER 18

WALKING ON STORMY SEAS

And Peter got out of the boat, and walked on the water and came
toward Jesus. But seeing the wind, he became frightened, and
beginning to sink, he cried out, "Lord, save me!"

—Matt. 14:29–30

After several months, Rusty approached me one day with concern in his eyes. "Mrs. Damoff, I love working for y'all, but I'm having a little problem with the agency."

"What's wrong?"

"Well . . ." He looked embarrassed. "They won't schedule me for more than thirty-nine hours a week. If I'm full time, they're supposed to offer me insurance benefits. And they don't want to do that."

"So, even though you're doing a great job, and the customer is happy, they're holding you back from full time?"

"Yes, ma'am, that's pretty much it. I'm frustrated, because I don't think my family can live off of what I can make there."

"I can't believe that!" My indignation rose as I considered the implications. "We don't want to lose you, Rusty. We'll have to figure something out."

Not long after Rusty shared his dilemma, I called the agency about an unrelated matter. I'd never received any statements reporting insurance payments made to them. The receptionist gave me a phone number for their business office, which was located in a different city. When I called, no one seemed to have access to the necessary files.

After several more attempts to obtain information, one person finally admitted a former employee had mishandled patient files and records of insurance payments. They would have to get back to me later. I waited a few weeks and called again but still received an evasive response. Our questions remained unanswered.

Faced with these actualities, George and I began to pray about taking a rather radical step: hiring Rusty ourselves. Insurance would not cover a private aide, but we could request funds for payment from Jacob's trust. After much consideration, checking with the managers of the trust, and discussion with Rusty, we decided this would be the best course for everyone concerned.

The home health agency resented our action, but they were too busy trying to sort out their business office chaos to interfere. They also knew they had mistreated Rusty. As a result, they lost our business and an excellent aide. Rusty completed his transactions with them in a nonconfrontational, respectful way, choosing to ignore the angry looks and accusing comments he received the last time he went to the office.

We were excited, not only to have Rusty, but to be able to treat him the way he deserved to be treated. We decided to pay him a salary instead of the hourly wages he'd been receiving. That way, even when our family left town for holidays, Rusty's pay would remain consistent. Based on the monthly amount Jacob's trust managers approved, we could afford to provide health insurance for Rusty and his family in addition to a pay increase.

The new arrangement proved ideal. Rusty already loved Jacob and had become like a part of our family. He could pour his heart into his work without worrying about the unfair practices of the agency. We had other reasons to be thankful as well. Knowing Rusty would be with Jacob at school each day comforted us.

School included its own set of trials.

I had attended regular meetings with the special ed department to review Jacob's instructional program. His steady recovery progress resulted in changes to his education plan each time we met. We wanted Jacob to enjoy meaningful peer interaction and exposure to real academic subject matter. With an aide there to take notes and assist, Jacob could be placed in more traditional classroom settings.

His schedule for the '97–'98 school year included three special ed subjects: math, English, and home economics. For mainstreaming purposes, the committee placed him in an eleventh-grade U.S. history class for half the year and a ninth-grade world history class for the second semester. A study period each day provided time for an aide to tutor Jacob and school therapists to work with him.

We welcomed the additional therapy. Julia Williams, an occupational therapist, offered valuable advice and insight. She helped Jacob to write, dress himself, and use a computer. Julia balanced gentleness and encouragement with determination. When Jacob said he couldn't do what she required, she kept pushing until he did it. Julia even came to our home to download spelling-tutor software on our computer, and she let us borrow other learning tools and devices.

The school therapists and some wonderful, compassionate teachers impressed us with their devotion to an often difficult calling. But we also encountered the occasional apathetic teacher who managed a room full of special ed kids like a glorified day care center. These teachers treated the students as though they had no potential for learning. A pervasive tendency toward low expectations discouraged us.

We hoped placing Jacob in regular classes would provide stimulation through socialization with his peers, even if he couldn't keep up with the academic requirements. However, problems quickly arose. Before the accident, Jacob had been an honor student in a private school, where his academic environment had consisted of intelligent discussions held in an atmosphere of respect. The mainstream classes Jacob now attended camped on the lowest rung of the intellectual ladder. Behavior issues swamped any academic efforts.

Physical fights often erupted. Yelling matches between students occurred daily, and verbal attacks on teachers were almost as common. Policemen visited the classroom on a regular basis. It was a war zone.

When Rusty became Jacob's full-time aide during the second semester, we relaxed somewhat, expecting him to be able to handle tutoring requirements and any potentially dangerous situation that might arise. Our false sense of security dissolved, though, when Rusty came home with Jacob one afternoon and told us the following story.

They'd been sitting in Jacob's mainstream history class when two students began shouting obscenities at each other. When the teacher attempted to intervene, the instigating student redirected her venom at the teacher. Physical violence appeared imminent, so the teacher used her electronic panic button to summon a policeman.

The officer arrived, apprehended the offending student to place her in "boot camp," and paused to issue a warning to the remaining students. Assuming a posture of stern authority, he barked, "Does anyone else want to go to boot camp?" Before Rusty realized what was happening, Jacob raised his hand.

"You think you're funny?" The officer yelled, red-faced at Jacob's impertinence. Rusty found his tongue and apologized, stumbling over his words in an attempt to explain that Jacob didn't fully understand what was going on. After glaring at Jacob for a long moment, the officer left with the other student, and Rusty heaved a sigh of relief.

As I imagined the whole scene in my mind, I had to laugh at the picture of Jacob raising his hand at such an inopportune moment. Rusty laughed, too, in retrospect. But we both realized Jacob needed to be removed from the dangers and negative influences he encountered in his current classes.

At the next review meeting, Rusty and I explained our position. We argued that Jacob's mainstream situation served only to accomplish the exact opposite of our stated goals. The regular classroom exposed Jacob to delinquent behavior instead of appropriate social interaction.

"You have a good point," the special ed department head agreed. "But our options are limited. We can place Jacob back in all special ed classes if you like."

I had come prepared for this moment. "We want Jacob to attend honors classes."

The school officials reacted with immediate strong opposition. "Honors students receive weighted credit," the department head reminded me. "It wouldn't be fair for Jacob to be included in that system."

I leaned forward. "I am not suggesting that Jacob receive honors credit. I know he can't handle the requirements of those courses. Our desire is to place Jacob in the midst of students who think and behave the way he used to."

I looked at each of the committee members present. Their set expressions and crossed arms told me they weren't convinced. "He's not disruptive," I continued. "And he won't interfere with the teachers or their students. He would simply be another person in the room, benefiting from the instruction and discussion taking place around him. Rusty would be there to help him stay focused, and he could always take Jacob out if he became a distraction."

The department head stared at me in silence for a moment. Then she shrugged. "Well, I guess it won't hurt to ask the teachers if they mind."

The teachers didn't mind at all, and Jacob joined an honors history class. The teacher not only welcomed him, she included him in class projects and discussions. Jacob began experiencing the kind of classroom environment we had envisioned for him when we first brought him back into the school system. As for the worst of what had transpired before, we just thanked God he'd survived it unharmed.

⋅•◈×◈•⋅

With Jacob's school situation in hand, a wonderful full-time aide, and God's generous financial provision, we hoped to settle into a pleasant, productive routine. As it turned out, we hadn't reached calm waters yet.

My friendship with Barton had continued to grow and deepen. During his second year as youth minister at Trinity Episcopal Church, he'd started a Tuesday night Bible study for high school students and asked me to help by leading worship with my guitar. Grace and Jacob both attended the meetings.

The Tuesday night event had been drawing a nice crowd for more than a year, and everything seemed to be going great. But all was not well. As Barton and I grew closer and spent more time together, jealousy seeped into George's heart. He knew he had encouraged the friendship, but accusing thoughts darkened his mind. He tried to suppress them, but then a well-meaning male friend told George he'd seen Barton and me walking together. Did George know what was "going on" between us?

George wouldn't explain his somber mood when I asked. For a long time he hoped to overcome his jealousy on his own, but it kept increasing until he could no longer hold it in. When the dam finally burst and he told me how he felt, I didn't know what to do. I understood George's feelings, but it seemed unfair to ditch Barton as a friend when he hadn't done anything wrong.

George didn't insist I end the friendship, but knowing he felt hurt and threatened grieved me. I knew I was wholeheartedly committed to my marriage. As much as we liked each other, neither Barton nor I desired a romantic relationship.

However, as I considered distancing myself from Barton for George's sake, I realized the friendship meant more to me than perhaps it should. And I had to admit I enjoyed the attention.

One evening George confronted me before I left for Tuesday night worship. "Would you be comfortable if I had a close female friend?"

"I think I'd be fine with it if she were twelve years older."

He shook his head. "Not if she didn't look it."

I couldn't argue that point. Though I was over forty, people often mistook me for being much younger. Like the time I delivered an assignment to Grace at the high school, and two teachers stopped me for my student hall pass.

Another humorous incident occurred the year after Jacob's accident, when he and I participated in a pro-life fund-raising event called "Walk for Life." Because Jacob had become a local celebrity of sorts, the *Marshall News Messenger* ran a photograph of us walking the mile around the downtown square. The photographer knew our family and included the caption, "Jacob Damoff and his mother, Jeanne." The copy editor who laid out the page looked at the picture, assumed it was an error, and changed "mother" to "sister."

Proud of my appearance, George had always enjoyed repeating comments his male college students made about me. One of his favorite
stories involved the time he and a freshman stood talking on the sidewalk in front of the science building at ETBU. I arrived with our kids,
pulling into a parking space a few feet away. Before I could get out of
the car, the student nudged George. "Hey, Mr. D., can I have your
babysitter's phone number?"

George had dryly said, "That's my wife."

I'd always basked in the admiration I saw in George's eyes when he
told that story. But compliments from other men didn't mix well with
his new insecurity. Phrases that once brought him pleasure now haunted
him and fueled his fears: "I saw you at the concert last night with your
daughter"; "Your wife looks hot in that baseball cap"; "How'd you get a
woman who looks like that to marry you?" If college-aged men found
me attractive, why wouldn't a thirty-year-old youth minister? George
trusted me, but he couldn't shut off his imagination. And he couldn't
stand where it kept taking him.

George and I both understood the immense emotional strain Jacob's
accident had placed on our marriage and family. We'd heard about
strong Christians succumbing to sexual temptation in search of comfort. Those stories intensified George's fears.

I knew the stories, too, but I wasn't tempted to search for comfort in
another man's arms. I already had a wonderful husband who loved me
more than I could begin to understand. Only a raving lunatic would
have risked losing him for anyone or anything. And yet, my actions
were wounding him.

I appreciated George's honest communication of his feelings. By
expressing his concerns, he made the issue *ours* instead of his alone,
helping fortify the wall protecting our marriage. I realized he could
have been angry and defensive, but he chose to draw near to me. We
both prayed for an outcome that would satisfy everyone. Even as I
prayed, I wondered if such an outcome existed.

Someone else had been praying for me, too. She hadn't told me, but
Pam Dowd had been asking God to protect me in my friendship with
Barton since he'd first entered the picture. About the same time George
expressed his struggles, Natalie told Pam seeing Barton and me together

worried her. "I know Mrs. Damoff is older, but she doesn't *look* older. That makes it weird. Do you think everything is OK?"

Being a true friend, Pam called and confronted me. She told me what Natalie had said. "I have to ask you this, Jeanne. Do you have a problem with him?"

I assured her I didn't and thanked her for holding me accountable. After I hung up, I pondered the conversation. More than anything, Natalie's concern burdened me. Was my friendship with Barton a stumbling block to the students we both ministered to?

I prayed for wisdom. George was battling jealousy, and people were asking questions. Even if nothing wrong had happened, I wanted to avoid the appearance of evil. An unpleasant choice presented itself: tell Barton I could no longer be his close friend, or risk damaging my marriage and ministry.

The answer seemed obvious. The more I prayed, the more I realized I'd let myself become too emotionally dependent on Barton. I would have to sever a bond that never should have become so strong. But how was I going to explain all this to Barton? As it turned out, I didn't have to.

A few weeks later, after three years in Marshall, Barton accepted a full-time teaching position in Houston. In a way I was sorry to see him go. Barton had been a great friend in my time of need. But mostly I felt relief. Friendship from a distance would be better for everyone.

After Barton moved, I apologized to George for giving Barton more attention than I should have. He forgave me. We both realized Barton's and my friendship had unfolded in a natural and innocent way, but it could have resulted in life-shattering consequences, had everyone involved not been committed to integrity and protected by a merciful God.

One afternoon, driving to a restaurant in Longview, Pam and I discussed the matter as well. Pulling into a space in the parking lot, she shifted into park, then turned to look at me. "I was very concerned for you, because of the stress you were under. Natalie and I both noticed you'd changed in some ways . . . mostly you'd been exercising more. I know you always stayed fit, but it seemed like after the accident, you took charge of what you could in life. Because so much was out of your control."

"I never thought about it that way. You may be right."

Pam leaned back in her seat. "I didn't see your behavior as unhealthy. My concern was that you looked even more youthful. You and Barton were spending so much time together, and you looked so good. And . . ." She paused.

"And what?"

Pam shot me a sheepish grin. "I was concerned for you and George, but I was also jealous of your friendship with Barton."

"Oh, Pam! I'm so sorry. You've been such an amazing friend to me. I never would have hurt you on purpose." I laid my hand on her arm. "Really, though, I would think you'd have been glad for a break! I imagine I wore you out with my neediness."

She smiled. "No. I missed you. You were *my* friend."

I used my best valley girl accent. "Gosh, I feel so popular."

Pam and I both laughed. I hugged her. "Thanks for your patience. And thanks so much for your prayers."

"Any time, friend."

That evening as I prepared dinner, I thought about my conversation with Pam and the way I'd hurt George. I felt ashamed and thankful at the same time. We'd escaped any permanent damage, but a sobering thought struck me. With all the prayer surrounding our family, how had these darts found a chink in the armor?

I remembered a verse. "Satan is like a roaring lion, seeking whom he may devour." Satan doesn't fight fair. Often, he takes something good—something God has done—and perverts it into an instrument of destruction. Barton was a great friend. Satan, the accuser of the brethren, used our friendship to stir up lies and jealousy. *Lord, help me be more guarded and discerning in the future.*

After the family had been seated for dinner, I scanned the faces around me: George, faithful servant to this family, sitting at the head of the table and at a place of honor in my heart; Grace, growing more beautiful and mature every day, secure in her faith, freed from former feelings of guilt; Luke, still the upbeat little brother, funny and smart, reminding me more and more of how Jacob had been before; and Jacob, concentrating so hard to lift a shaky fork to his mouth. A miracle.

George glanced at me. "Are you crying?"

I laughed. "No. Well, yes. I'm just thankful we're all here together. As a family."

CHAPTER 19

A PEBBLE FOUND

God sees not as man sees, for man looks at the outward appearance,
but the LORD *looks at the heart.*

—1 Sam. 16:7

Over the course of Jacob's gradual recovery, we observed his blossoming personality traits with a mixture of anticipation and apprehension. Based on doctor's warnings and the behavior we witnessed in other patients at Baylor Rehab, we prepared ourselves to endure stages of violence or obscenity. God, in His great mercy, spared us anything of that nature. Jacob emerged as a fascinating combination of who he had been before and an altogether new creation.

The Jacob we'd known and loved returned to us in some respects. But obvious differences exist, too. One of the more humorous changes involves tidiness. Before his injury, Jacob lived happily amid chaotic disarray. Now he displays a compulsion for order.

Anything Jacob considers trash receives his immediate and thorough attention. A scrap of paper. A thread on the arm of a chair. A microscopic crumb of food. No matter how small or insignificant, Jacob fixates on it until he's disposed of it. Sometimes this tendency becomes a nuisance. If we try to take Jacob for a walk, he stops every few feet to pick up a candy wrapper or cigarette butt. He even pauses to remove fallen leaves, one by one, from the sidewalk.

Before Natalie left for college, she turned this obsession into a useful activity and a way to spend time with Jacob. She'd walk Jacob through the neighborhood, allowing him to pick up all the trash he found and put it in a garbage bag. Once, while Natalie was distracted, Jacob picked up a dead bird and brought it to her for the bag. She learned to pay closer attention.

Another amusing change is Jacob's taste in fashion. Just to see what he'll say, I sometimes offer him ridiculous clothing combinations—not at all far removed from what he wore before—and he laughs like I've lost my mind. His current wardrobe consists mostly of khakis and simple styles in neutral or muted tones. Mountain-climbing pants with elastic in the waist and pullover shirts make self-dressing easier for Jacob. With his limited fine-motor skills, buttons and snaps remain a challenge.

Evidence indicates other parts of Jacob's past are still lurking in the recesses of his brain, waiting for the right stimulation to call them forth. Musical interests remain strong. We also noticed a quiet soberness in Jacob's expression one day while he watched skateboarding on television.

"Jacob, do you remember skateboarding?"

A wistful look accompanied his soft, "Yeah."

Little by little, memories of former abilities and their contrast to current limitations have awakened. But in a benevolent, ironic twist, Jacob's brain injury heals the wounds it creates. His short-term memory is such that he soon forgets what has upset him.

In spite of all he has lost, Jacob is happy most of the time. Crying came back for a cleansing season and then stopped altogether, but laughter remains a constant delight. When something amuses Jacob, he laughs with total abandon. And it doesn't take much to amuse him. Joy bubbles just below the surface and seems to infect everyone around him.

God uses Jacob to teach us profound lessons in simple living. Sometimes, in frustration, we utter the rhetorical question, "Who knows?"

Jacob immediately answers, "God." He reminds us God is in control of whatever circumstances we're allowing to rattle us.

Jacob also demonstrates a deep respect for God's creation. When George works in the yard, he often enlists Jacob's help with the easier tasks. Once, as George raked leaves into piles, Jacob picked them up by handfuls and placed them in a wheelbarrow. As he scooped up some leaves, he inadvertently picked a few blades of grass. Jacob looked down at the green blades in his hand and said, "Sorry, God."

George stopped raking. "Why are you telling God you're sorry?"

Jacob responded with true remorse in his eyes and voice. "The grass was alive."

Upon hearing this story, a friend of mine commented, "Jacob could be St. Francis' brother!"

Always on the lookout for signs of the old Jacob, any evidence of his former personality delights us. Even traits that got on our nerves before, we embrace warmly when they recur. At first, that is.

Several years after Jacob's injury, we visited some of George's relatives in Ohio. While there, George and Grace took Jacob for a walk through an overgrown field. After going a short distance, Jacob froze in his tracks and shouted, "Shoot me now!"

George and Grace couldn't imagine what had prompted the outburst. After asking a few questions, they realized the stiff grass was scraping against his bare lower legs. Welcome back, melodrama! For a few months, Jacob used his shoot-me-now phrase whenever something upset him. We learned to ignore it, just as we had ignored his overreactions in childhood. On occasion, however, uninitiated observers raised an eyebrow when we showed no alarm as Jacob begged to be put out of his misery.

Eventually, Jacob shortened his standard complaint to, "Pain!" This handy catch-all word proved suitable for any unpleasant situation, from irritation over his sister's playful teasing to real physical pain. In most cases, however, the verbal explosion far exceeded the injury. Jacob's over-the-top theatrics amuse us. Thankfully, he never stays upset for long. His cheerful disposition almost always returns within moments of the "crisis."

Jacob has progressed through a series of pet words and phrases, each lasting for a time and then fading away. Some of them have been quite ingenious. Case in point: When any item goes missing, Jacob's trash obsession makes him a prime suspect. During one particular phase, if I asked, "Jacob, did you throw away the shopping list I placed on the counter?" he would think for a moment, then answer, "Never on purpose."

A declaration of absolute certainty. With a safety hatch. He would make a great politician.

Though he remastered the art of overreaction, for a long time Jacob remained blissfully ignorant when it came to anticipating pain. The first time I took him to the dentist after his injury, several small cavities required attention. I sat across the room as the doctor filled them. With several people hovering over him, the drill whirring, and tooth dust flying, I could see Jacob's hands folded in his lap, perfectly relaxed. The mental aspect of pain no longer tormented him.

However, in 2002, six years post injury, a dermatologist prescribed Accutane to treat Jacob's complexion problems. Because of potential harmful side effects, the treatment required monthly blood tests at the hospital. During Jacob's fourth visit to the lab, the phlebotomist prepared to insert the needle as usual. Jacob suddenly flinched and pulled away. "I'm so scared!"

I doubt many mothers have been more pleased to see their son recoil in fear. The next time we went, while we were still in the outpatient waiting room, he leaned toward me and whispered, "I'm so scared of that needle."

Any observer would have thought me heartless. Though I assured him everything would be fine, I couldn't stop smiling as I considered the implications of his confession. Like ever-widening ripples, progress may have become more difficult to discern, but it hadn't stopped.

The ripples that began on a warm May afternoon in 1996 persist, exerting their silent but steady influence. Despite Jacob's simple, quiet lifestyle, God continues to work in and through him, touching many.

"See You at the Pole" is a national movement to promote student-led prayer vigils in public schools. On one predetermined morning, students gather around their school's flagpole before classes begin to pray for their campuses, teachers, administrators, and friends. Local youth groups work together to promote and lead the event.

Area churches often organize a community-wide youth meeting as a follow-up event on the same evening. In the autumn of 1997, our church hosted the event. Almost all the churches in Marshall, and many of their youth groups, had prayed for Jacob faithfully during the early, critical months of his ordeal. Some of the students present at the meeting had been involved in the yellow ribbon campaign.

Sue Werner asked me if Stephanie Hillhouse, one of the girls in our youth group, could share specific details about how God had worked in Jacob's life. Sue believed an update would encourage and bless the students.

As part of our church praise band, I helped lead the worship music for the service. I watched with joy as Stephanie took Jacob's hand and guided him to the front of the room. Hundreds of local teens listened in silence as she gave glory to God for Jacob's healing and presence among them. She held his hand as she spoke, and turned to face him as she finished her testimony. "Here he is, standing before all of us who prayed for him, able to walk, able to speak, able to give praise to the Lord. Isn't that right, Jacob?"

I've never seen that large a group of teens so hushed and still. Looking a little sheepish and overwhelmed, Jacob shyly answered, "Yeah."

The students erupted in shouts and turbulent applause, as Jacob stood smiling beside Stephanie. Tears rolled down my cheeks. Tears of gratitude for God's mercy and power in using a broken boy to advance His kingdom.

The next spring Sue told me Stephanie Hillhouse had visited Jacob every day during the time he'd stayed at Merritt Plaza. For the entire eight months, she hadn't missed a single day, and no one had ever told us. She graduated that year, and in her senior pictures, a delicate gold chain hangs around her neck. A small, gold safety pin filled with yellow beads dangles from the chain. The reminder to pray for Jacob.

After George and I learned I was pregnant with Jacob, we discussed various names we liked for boys and girls. One day I read Isaiah 27:6: "In the days to come Jacob will take root, Israel will blossom and sprout, and they will fill the whole world with fruit."

As soon as I read the verse, I knew. This baby was a boy, and his name was Jacob. There just didn't seem to be any other option. A glorious assurance filled me. God had plans for Jacob. He would make Jacob's life fruitful.

Never would I have imagined God's plan included a path of suffering for Jacob and our family. No mother in her right mind prays her child will face tragedy and grow up to be a brain-injured, dependent young man who can't write his own name without assistance. But Jacob is bearing much fruit for eternity. He possesses a unique beauty that draws everyone around him into the presence of God.

The Lord, in His wisdom, doesn't tell us what our future holds. But He does prepare us for what lies ahead, and He goes before us into the plans He has ordained. Jacob hasn't been ruined. He is still becoming exactly what God wants him to be.

Though we as humans place great value on intellect and worldly success, there's only one way to delight the heart of God: worship. A gift from a lover's heart to the Beloved. All who approach God's throne clothed in His righteousness are equal, from the most brilliant scientist to the severely handicapped child.

The believer who offers the purest worship is the one who pleases the Lord most. But many of us don't want to appear fanatical, or perhaps we just don't want to attract attention to ourselves. When we worship among others, we're concerned about their opinions. Our focus is divided.

Jacob doesn't suffer from these afflictions. He worships with freedom and abandon. In church, he closes his eyes and lifts his hands to the sky, "singing" the songs, many of which remain in his memory from years gone by. His vocal control is minimal, and the words sound more like shouting than music. But they come from the heart of a lover.

One couple in our church left for a few months to lead music in another local congregation. Shortly after they returned, our pastor asked the husband to stand and share about their experiences in ministry. As the man concluded his remarks, he expressed how thankful they were to be back in our midst. Then tears sprang up in his eyes. "But the thing I missed most was watching Jacob Damoff worship."

Natalie Dowd's twin sister, Abigail, came by our house while home from college for a weekend. Energetic and fun-loving, she burst into the den to visit with Jacob. But when she saw him, she froze in her tracks.

Jacob loves Christian music videos, and over the years we've collected a few. At one point during a live Third Day concert, the band is leading their audience in singing, "I Have Decided to Follow Jesus." Abigail watched in awed silence as Jacob, standing in front of his chair, eyes closed, hands lifted high, poured out the words of utter, unreserved commitment: "No turning back; no turning back."

Touched to the core, Abigail left the den quietly and came to me with tears in her eyes. "I can't tell you what that did to me. His closeness to the Lord . . . it's amazing!"

I had to smile. Abigail's not often at a loss for words. But Jacob affects many people that way. Even strangers. There's a power in Jacob's innocence—a freedom in his abandonment that people see and wish they had.

If someone smiles at Jacob during church, he lights up in a huge grin and waves. He's not disruptive, and he always whispers to George or me if he has something to say. But he's not in bondage to a false sense of decorum either. Jacob enjoys the liberty of a child of God, one who is securely nestled in the arms of his Father. I never hear anyone say, "Poor Jacob." Jacob is not poor. "Blessed are the pure in heart, for they shall see God." Jacob is rich.

Within the first year after Jacob's accident, a friend from Virginia called to express her concern and love for our family. As we talked, she confessed, "The truth is, it really bothers me that this happened to Jacob, because you pray for your kids more than anyone I know. And God didn't protect him. What does that mean for the rest of us?"

I sensed the depth of her fear. Her only son was just a toddler. I answered her with honest conviction. "As strange as it sounds, how do we know God *didn't* protect Jacob? His thoughts and ways are higher than ours. I don't know why God chose for this to happen, but I have to believe He has reasons. Loving, good reasons. I still believe God is in control, and I also believe He answers all my prayers for my children according to His wisdom and purposes."

At the time, I meant every word, but still ached with loss and longed for understanding. As the years unfolded, I continued asking God to show me how Jacob's brain injury could be His plan. Then one day, as I poured out my heart in prayer for Jacob, it was as though God asked me a question.

"What has always been your heart's deepest prayer for your children?"

I knew the answer. "That, when they stand in Your presence, they will hear You say, 'Well done, good and faithful servant.'"

"Jacob loves Me with all his heart, soul, mind, and strength. He inspires others to love Me, too. Jacob is a good and faithful servant."

Joy flooded my heart as an amazing truth dawned. Jacob is indeed great in the kingdom of God. He may never impress the world with his accomplishments, but he delights the One who created him for His glory. What more could I ask for my son?

EPILOGUE:
NEVER-ENDING RIPPLES

*For I am confident of this very thing, that He who began a good
work in you will perfect it until the day of Christ Jesus.*
—Phil. 1:6

AUTUMN, 2007

The youth groups' yellow ribbon campaign produced a lasting effect on people of all ages. In downtown Marshall, where a historic courthouse stands in the middle of the town square, yellow ribbons adorned the trees that line the brick streets. The ribbons remained for years. Each winter, when city workers decorated the whole square with garlands and lights for Christmas, they left the ribbons in place. Time and the effects of weather eventually wore them to tatters, but only then were they removed. The ribbon Kirk and Sue Werner brought to us at Baylor Rehab remains on a shelf in Jacob's room.

Several years after Jacob's accident, Debbie Boatright-Camacho performed at a Baylor Rehab Christmas party. The family of a current patient knew Debbie and asked her to come. Though it's not a holiday song, Debbie felt "Jacob's Song" would be the perfect choice. She had no idea Jacob had ever been there. When she shared the story behind the song, Baylor Rehab staff members exchanged glances. "Could she be talking about *our* Jacob?" They summoned Dr. Carlile to the room and asked Debbie to repeat the song. Dr. Carlile listened with tears in her eyes. Baylor Rehab adopted "Jacob's Song" for use in therapy. Through Debbie's CD, the song has sent ripples around the world.

Jacob graduated from Marshall High School in May, 2001. As was only fitting, Rusty helped Jacob manage the stairs and walked across the stage with him. We teased Rusty, saying he should receive a diploma, too, for all the hours he spent at the school.

Grace graduated the same year, third in her class of 350 students. The following autumn, having received a generous scholarship, she began her freshman year in a scholars program at Seattle Pacific University. She graduated with honors in June of 2005 with degrees in Christian theology and European studies: Spanish.

During the summer of 2006, Grace began noticing stiffness and soreness in her joints. Her symptoms progressed rapidly, and doctors soon diagnosed the cause as rheumatoid arthritis, an autoimmune illness that can cripple and cause excruciating pain.

My immediate reaction was panic. "No, God! You can't let this happen to her. Please, don't let her suffer. Take it away."

In His mercy, God quieted my thoughts and reminded me of all we'd been through with Jacob. "You know I am good," my heart heard Him say. "If I give this to her, it is a gift."

I realized then that the truths we'd learned on our journey with Jacob were deeply rooted and unshakable. And I rejoiced to see Grace responding to her physical trial with trust in God's wisdom and provision. Had she not been through the flood with her brother, I wonder if she would have gained solid ground so quickly.

So far she is responding to chemo-type drugs and looking into more holistic options and lifestyle adjustments with the hope of discontinuing medication. And of course we continue to pray for healing. Thanks to God's amazing grace, peace reigns over the process.

On September 15, 2007, Grace married Curtis Romjue, a gifted musician and beautiful soul. Grace performs with Curtis's Seattle-based band, Jubilee (livejubilee.org), a registered 501(c)(3) non-profit organization that donates 10 percent of all booking fees and 50 percent of all merchandise sales to the International Justice Mission (ijm.org).

Grace lives life with joyful abandon, soaks up knowledge, and possesses an uncommon depth of maturity and compassion. In all these aspects, Curtis is her perfect complement. Together they strive to open their hearts and home to serve God, each other, and their community.

In the fall of 2003, Luke left home to attend Wheaton College in Illinois. He graduated in May, 2007, with degrees in philosophy and English. A poet, musician, and deep thinker, Luke greets life with the same expectancy he possessed as a child. Currently serving as a midterm missionary with World Venture in Cote d'Ivoire, Africa, Luke approaches his faith in God with the passion of an artist (ldamoff. blogspot.com).

I've never met anyone who doesn't like Luke. Sometimes he'll say or do something that sparks a memory of Jacob before the accident, and I wonder, if Jacob hadn't drowned, would he have developed many of the same gifts as Luke? But then I remind myself there is no alternate reality. No "what might have been."

As Jacob's sister and brother launch out into the adult world, he remains dependent and may always require the services of a caretaker. Jacob spends weekdays in the country at Rusty's house. They work in the garden, take care of cattle, paint fences, and do other chores. Jacob still struggles to maintain his balance on uneven terrain and can't handle stairs without assistance. But he has learned to dress, feed himself, and work simple electronic devices like a DVD player or microwave. Rusty continues to tutor Jacob in math and reading.

Though his speech is still somewhat slurred, Jacob's observations often reveal a deeply thoughtful mind and keen perception about people and God. His joy seems to well up from a perpetual spring. God's law is written on his heart. I still wonder sometimes what he sees when he closes his eyes to worship.

In June of 2003, Natalie Dowd married Wade Grubbs. George, Grace, and I provided music in the wedding. Dressed in a suit and tie, Jacob sat beside the aisle in the second pew. As Natalie entered the church on her father's arm, she paused beside Jacob and hugged him. He smiled and returned her hug.

On July 3, 2007, Natalie gave birth to her first child, a boy. She named him Lawson Jacob, keeping a promise she'd made to her best friend more than a decade ago.

Jacob enjoys rich relationships with family and friends. He lives, laughs, loves, and worships from the heart. And Jacob's story isn't over. Each sunrise brings new adventures and challenges. Though some days seem to offer nothing beyond the tedium of the routine, the Lord's mercies never cease. They are new every morning.

If I said I never grieve anymore, I'd be lying. Sometimes I look at Jacob and sorrow washes over me as I think about the way he was before. But I've learned not to stay in that place long. Jacob is on the path God has chosen for him. We travel alongside, gasping at the glimpses of glory we see when the veil lifts for a moment. God's purpose. Plans formed long ago with perfect faithfulness. And God is able to bring them to pass. Of all that God has spoken concerning Jacob, not one word will fail.

Ripples widen. As they diminish over time, we may hardly notice them any more. But the ripples don't stop. Not until they reach the shore.

APPENDIX A:

IN THEIR OWN WORDS

Men shall speak of the power of Your awesome acts, and I will tell of Your greatness.

—Ps. 145:6

It's one thing for me to say God brought amazing beauty out of our tragedy, touching many people and changing their lives forever. A skeptical reader could dismiss the claim as the biased opinion of a doting mother.

But what if the people whose lives were changed speak for themselves? This appendix contains testimonies from individuals, many of whom you'll recognize as "characters" in the story. As you read their powerful words, listen for the sound of ripples.

Pam Dowd (Jeanne's friend)

The phone call came as I was planning a shopping trip with my daughters, Natalie, Abigail, and Lindsay. In the seconds it took me to reach the receiver, my family's life changed forever.

Before I could say hello, a breathless Philip Jones said, "Pam, I know how close you are to the Damoffs." Philip's voice cracked, and I knew something was terribly wrong. I'd seen Philip in stressful situations before, and he'd never sounded like this. Then he said the words I still can't believe: "Jacob drowned."

I felt as if I'd been dropped from a very tall building. I grabbed the dresser to stay upright.

Philip continued before I could catch my breath. "He must have been under the water fifteen minutes before we found him. We've tried everything. We're doing CPR, but we can't get him to breathe. Jacob's dead. I found him, but . . . I was too late."

My hand flew to my open mouth. Then, when I didn't think the pain could get worse, he added, "Jeremy Maxey's still missing. We're looking for him. I've got to go."

Two dead on a school trip? It couldn't be. I knew the staff. I'd been Trinity's principal for almost eight years. I turned to walk into the next room, searching for words to describe such horrible news to my fifteen-year-old twins and my ten-year-old. Natalie was Jacob's best friend. Abigail thought she'd marry Jacob someday. Grace and Lindsay played together often.

I can still hear Natalie and Abigail's wails of terror like they're echoing in a dream I can't wake from. Lindsay, so young at the time, started to cry as the four of us dropped to our knees in the game room, clinging to each other, to offer immediate prayers to the only One who understood what was going on. We certainly didn't.

We prayed the only words we could find. "No! No! Help Jacob and Jeremy. Dear God, no! Please don't let this happen. Protect them, God. Help the teachers and parents find Jeremy. Let them live. Revive Jacob, Lord. Please help us. Be with Jeanne, George, Grace, and Luke as they find out."

We couldn't think of anything else to say, so we said it all again.

This was supposed to be a fun day. A beginning-of-summer kind of day filled with laughter and lightheartedness. It had become a nightmare. The phone rang again, and we stared at it with dread. I ran to pick it up. The girls clustered around me.

A breathless Philip said, "He's breathing, Pam. Jacob's breathing. Praise God! He's blue, but he's alive." I could hear the ambulance siren in the background.

We'll never understand why Jeremy had to die that day, and we grieved for his family, but we had found a tiny window of hope in the tragedy. God had answered our desperate prayers for Jacob. Surely He would answer those we said as we rushed toward the hospital.

I tried to prepare the girls as we drove. I didn't know what it would mean for Jacob to have been dead for so long, but I knew it couldn't be good. Natalie and Abigail, on the other hand, were elated he was breathing and fully expected Jacob to be recovered by evening. We arrived before the ambulance to find about a hundred students, teachers, friends, and family gathered in small circles—clinging, crying, and praying for the nightmare to end.

When they ushered Jeanne through the emergency room doors, I thought I'd die. I couldn't imagine being Jacob's mother. She looked so pale and fragile. She didn't focus on anyone as her eyes searched for George. When he came to take her to Jacob, I breathed my first sigh of relief. At least she could hold him, and surely he'd wake up now that she was there and he was breathing again. We knew so little about anoxic brain injury back then.

I don't remember eating for the first three weeks. I think I lost ten or more pounds. Normal daily activities seemed meaningless when I could be helping Jeanne and George, assuring they got some rest, and taking care of details such as sitting with Jacob, answering the never-ending phone calls in the ICU waiting room, and fielding the constant questions from the crowd of friends and family gathered to wait for Jacob to emerge from coma.

Nothing seemed important except sitting with Jacob, singing to him, quoting Scripture, and praying over him. My husband, Rodney, took care of things at home. I spent my waking hours filling whatever need I could, and yet I still felt helpless—as if I couldn't do enough to buffer the constant pain around the Damoff family.

Through trips back and forth to ICU, to Dallas and Baylor Rehab, on daily visits to the nursing home, and eventually to Jacob's house, I learned we serve a faithful God who supplies our needs one at a time—neither too soon nor too late. His timing is perfect.

I had never considered God's eternal sovereignty much before Jacob drowned to live again. But after many hours of walking through Jacob's fragile, damaged world, trying to glimpse God's perspective, while Jacob's life pages turned to reveal yet another miracle, I came to believe

God has a plan for every circumstance we encounter. It's undeniable, unchangeable, and unshakable. He is neither surprised by the events of our lives nor by our choices.

God is not at our whim, though He allows us to beckon and call. He teaches us how to pray answerable prayers. He is sovereign, Yahweh, our healer and provider. It is when we trust Him that He can begin to unfold the plans He created specifically for us.

Jacob's story has not ended. It is but a drop in the pond of God's eternal provision for us all. God used Jacob to capture our attention in a way that didn't exist before the accident. Jacob's life speaks volumes to my soul. God is trustworthy and sovereign. He understands dying and living again!

Fear not, He beckons our quavering hearts as we stare into an uncertain future. *I always have a plan.*

"'For I know the plans I have for you,' declares the LORD, 'plans to prosper you and not to harm you, plans to give you hope and a future. Then you will call upon me and come and pray to me, and I will listen to you. You will seek me and find me when you seek me with all your heart. I will be found by you,' declares the LORD" (Jer. 29:11–14 NIV).

Grace Damoff Romjue (Jacob's sister)

Before the accident, Jacob was a force to be reckoned with. I was actually afraid of him for most of my childhood. But I loved him more deeply than I feared him. I adored him, like children look upon their favorite heroes and role models with upturned faces and eyes filled with awe.

I couldn't understand him with his passions and volatile, often violent emotions, with his determined mind that could not be swayed. He was so independent and so strong. He could always stand on his own, and he was always the trailblazer. He had a charisma that drew all kinds of people to him. People admired and respected him for his individuality. People not only wanted to be around him, they wanted to *be* him.

I remember I used to love going into his room on those rare occasions when he would let me. There was so much of him that I didn't understand: his artwork, his music, the way he dressed, the girls he liked. I was always trying to get glimpses inside his world to try to unravel all the mysteries that seemed to surround him.

Even though he was my brother, he seemed so distant from me much of the time. Luke and I had always been playmates as children, content to spend our time in the house, the backyard, or the neighborhood. Jacob was cut out of an entirely different cloth. It seemed as if he was always pushing the boundaries of his world farther and farther outward, blazing trails into the unknown. Little did any of us know how much he would need this strength and independence to endure the trials he would have to face.

When I first imagined I would have to live the rest of my life without Jacob, I felt so inadequate to be the new oldest sibling—to try to fill Jacob's role in our family. I wasn't ready to be the first to do everything, to be the trailblazer that he had always been. I couldn't imagine getting my driver's license, graduating from high school, leaving for college, getting married—without having seen him do it first. There was no possible way to imitate his charisma. I wasn't a trendsetter like he was.

Then I thought about how I was never going to be able to explain to other people who he had been to me—what a strong personality he had, all the elements of his sense of humor, his intellectual brilliance, his mysterious aloofness, and his contagious energy. This is the person I had spent my childhood admiring. I had walked in his shadow, counted on him to show me how so many challenging things could be done. I could not have imagined at the time of my greatest grief that he would show me—through his tragedy—how to conquer even greater challenges than getting a driver's license and leaving for college.

Jacob became a new person in my life after his accident. He played a different role than the big brother I had known as a child. But he continues to be the big brother whose strength of personality and overwhelming passion and energy cause me to admire him as a child admires a hero.

I have gained so many things from Jacob. He was an inspiration to me from my earliest years, and he continues to be my inspiration. If ever I have seen God's restorative work it has been in Jacob's life— renewing him through death and suffering to be a person who now draws people to him, not through his own uniqueness, but through an innocent simplicity that directs others' eyes to heaven. Jacob had this gift even before his accident.

Across the top of the doorframe exiting his bedroom he had a sign that read "Today is the greatest day and I am in it," with a small drawing of three crosses on a hill. In college I placed an identical sign over my dorm-room door, and as I exited into the world each day, I was not only reminded of Jacob—his passion and fearlessness—but I was reminded of the beauty that God is able to accomplish in each day because we have life and creativity and passion and boldness through Him.

Luke Damoff (Jacob's brother)

It is almost as if all my memories have been made into an independent film, and I watch them at various speeds with some of the scenes deleted. I remember Mr. Godinich, my best friend Cody's dad, telling me Jacob was hospitalized. I can hear Cody as the elevator doors opened asking what "ICU" stood for. Then I'm running down the hall to my father, crying tears of frightened ignorance. I don't remember him telling me anything. I just remember finally knowing the truth and wishing somehow it was six hours earlier when my brother was normal and greeted me with "Hey, stupid."

I can see the chapel in the ICU with its wood-paneled walls and warm yellow light shining on the dark brown and deep red of the kneeling rails and pews. I remember my father taking me there and telling me that Jeremy was dead. I can hear that word ringing hollow in my head and feel its crashing into me with realization. I cried with Cody. Blind with tears; crying, not for my brother, but for Jeremy.

I can see the students in swimsuits. Hair still wet with lake water, cheeks streaked with saline. I feel the crush of a thousand hugs from faceless weeping people. I remember the comfort. The aluminum pans of food made by widows. Each meal had a different signature, instead of the consistency of my mother's cooking.

I stayed with my cousins on their farm that summer, and then later with my grandparents in Dallas. I remember the distraction and not seeing my brother for weeks at a time. I remember the tangible silence of not talking about what was always on our minds. This is what I remember.

I am unsure how to precisely assess how this has affected me. I never experienced being a teenager without having had a tragedy occur. I don't ever recall hating God, though I recall being angry. I don't recall being forced to grow up quickly, though looking back I know I was— not by any will of my parents but by the circumstances surrounding the life I was led to. I don't recall a conscious decision to get up and face every day, though I made them every time I got out of bed in the months and years that followed.

I do recall being embarrassed at the sort of pitied fame that only a small town can give its unfortunate members. I recall not feeling like I deserved or earned pity, and I distinctly recall not wanting it. I always felt normal, and I still feel sorry for families with disabled children, even though I suppose I am a part of one. I guess I still believe it will never happen to me, even though it already has.

I should say how God was merciful throughout this whole ordeal. For He was exceedingly merciful. Every breath given was mercy and grace. Every meal cooked was mercy and grace. The strength to rise every morning and lie back down at night was mercy and grace. The unwillingness to roll over and give up was mercy and grace.

That God has used and will continue to use this for His glory is the ultimate mercy. And that He has allowed and will continue to allow my family's trials to glorify Him is the ultimate grace. It is impossible for me to fully know or understand just how my brother's accident has brought and will continue to bring glory to the Lord, but I am assured that it has and it will continue to. I have seen a little, and heard a little more, of the stories of people positively affected by my brother's drowning. But even in my ignorance I have learned to accept and love the fate God has given my family and all of those who know and love my brother.

I still wonder why it must be this way. I still grieve when I see my brother sometimes. I wonder what he would be like, what kind of man he would be if he had been given a chance to live a normal life. I still get angry at times, thinking about the brilliant mind that is so damaged.

But I am constantly humbled by the words of Job: "The LORD gave, and the LORD has taken away; blessed be the name of the LORD."

My father taught me from a young age to hold everything with an open hand—to accept what was given graciously and to be willing to give it up just as graciously if it was asked or required. If we are to hold everything with an open hand, we must hold on to our family the same way. And though we may wish and pray and hope that God's will allows for them long life and prosperity, we must also be willing to accept the alternative, for everything is the Lord's, and all was made for His glory. He never promised us ease, but He promised us comfort.

I have learned through this to glorify God in all things—to praise His name in the very worst of times. Not for my comfort but for His glory. I have learned to joyfully accept the things God gives. Maybe not happily, but with joy. For I have been promised that, while it may not be easy, it will work out for good, if I truly love Christ and seek to glorify Him. What this has taught me, and continues to teach me every day, is that I must say at all times, "Blessed be the name of the LORD."

Sharon Miller (Jeanne's sister, Jacob's aunt)

Jacob was the first child to be born to my siblings—an adorable, curly-headed blond boy. He became the hero to my firstborn, Nathan, as they were growing up. An independent, fun-loving child, all his cousins adored him. On the day of his accident, my faith was shaken down to its roots. Tragedies were for other people, not my family! I felt helpless and out of control. We all hoped for an instant miracle—something quick and easy so we could get our lives back to normal. It was not to be. God wanted to take us deeper.

I have always been a wimp when it comes to pain or suffering. I hate hospitals, and nursing homes make me physically ill. But spending time there with someone you love changes your perspective. Now when I see people in wheelchairs, I look them in the eye and smile at them. That could be my nephew. That is a real person with real feelings. Funny how we can ignore such an idea until it hits close to home. My attitude toward sick or disabled people will never be the same.

The main thing I have come to realize is that we don't get to pick what happens to us or our children or our spouses. I am responsible to walk in obedience to God, but He is sovereign. He alone sees my life in its context of eternity, and He alone can call the shots according to His perfect plan. This is a very sobering thought for a control freak like me. But it is also a freeing thought. God has it all worked out. My job is to learn to trust Him.

I have seen how God pours out His grace on those who need it. Watching Jeanne and George deal with this situation has strengthened my faith that God's grace really is sufficient. Their lives are not ruined. Their marriage is intact and stronger than ever. It is a blessing to be around Jacob—he is sweet and wonderful and funny. He is handsome and genuine. He is still Nathan's hero, and an example to us all.

Nathan Miller (Jacob's cousin)

It was May of 1996, and I was twelve years old. My dad picked me up from baseball practice. He always forgot to bring me water, and this time I drank some of his Diet Coke. I never really liked the taste of Diet Coke. Halfway through the drive home he said he had something to tell me. My cousin Jacob had been in an accident.

Jacob was not my *real* best friend, because we hadn't lived in the same town since early childhood. Jacob had two siblings who were both closer to my age than he was. He was fifteen, learning to play the guitar and skateboarding. He wore clothes from Goodwill and a chain wallet. He was everything I wanted to be, and I adored him.

I don't know why he liked me as much as he did. Maybe it's because I was the cousin closest to his age. Maybe it's because I loved being around him, and would gladly be his interim best friend at any and all family functions. We were always sad on holidays when our families went to different places. At least, I was always sad, and I know that one time I heard someone else say that Jacob had been upset when we couldn't be together one Thanksgiving. That filled me with joy.

Knowing he loved me was one of the closest things on earth I've ever felt to the love of God. I knew he loved me, and I didn't know why. I only knew that I hadn't done anything to deserve it, and I certainly wasn't cool enough or funny enough or *anything* enough for him to want to be around me. Not that I thought Jacob was like God or anything. I just felt so honored to be loved by him at all.

And we had always had a blast together. Forming driveway hockey leagues and taking on his little brother's small group of friends, joking in the car on long trips, playing in the elevators during my sister's ballet recital, hunting for golf balls, roller-blading off of things and sometimes into things, singing songs from Disney movies and Christian rock bands. I counted the days until our families would next rendezvous. Getting out of baseball practice on that day in 1996, two days before school let out, I was already excited that his family was coming in that weekend for my sister's ballet recital.

When my dad mentioned an accident, I didn't know what he meant. I thought maybe Jacob had broken an arm or something. I sipped Diet Coke in the car as my dad explained to me that the Damoffs would not be coming to see us this weekend. He said Jacob had nearly drowned, and that he was in the hospital, and that he hadn't woken up yet. I was upset that he wouldn't be able to come see me that weekend. I hoped he would wake up soon so they could come anyway.

When I got home, my mom was in her room crying. I wasn't sure why, because at twelve years old, I wasn't sure if something bad had happened or not. But when she looked at me, I knew she expected me to cry, too. That's when I knew things were bad.

I saw Jacob in the hospital that weekend. His hair was long, and he was hooked up to all kinds of machines. My mom had always said she was going to cut his hair sometime while he was sleeping.

I don't know how many days passed before it began to dawn on me that he might not wake up. I knew he had to. The possibility that he wouldn't was absurd to me. I had never had a close relative die or anything like that. Jacob would wake up, and when he did we would be skateboarding within a few hours.

I cried that summer. A lot of times. Sometimes because I was scared, sometimes because I missed him, sometimes because the anxiety of waiting for him to wake up needed to flood out of my system. But I never grieved. He was always alive, three hours away at a hospital in Dallas. Inside of his living person was a mind that knew the code words to a hundred of our stupid clubs, a mind that could think of the cleverest comebacks every time, a mind that had thousands of memories very similar to my own, only his were documented from a slightly higher elevation and often faster speeds. So I always had hope that he would just wake up.

At some point in the middle of the summer, my mom came up to me while I was practicing basketball in the driveway. Some doctor had said that Jacob would be a vegetable for the rest of his life, she told me. I can't remember if she cried then. I know I did. Right there in my driveway. My child's mind had existed day to day until that point, always on the hope and prayer that he would wake up. And now some expert was sure enough that he wouldn't to bluntly announce the fact to his parents and anyone who might happen to love him.

It was God's grace that kept me together. Shortly afterward, I heard some amazing news. Again, my mom was the one who told me. My uncle George, Jacob's dad, had been holding Jacob's hand. He had asked him to squeeze his hand, and he had. I was elated beyond belief when I heard. It was as though God had made it clear to me that Jacob could have been taken away completely, and then in His infinite goodness, He began to give him back.

Within the following weeks and months Jacob began to respond to people more and more. His brother, Luke, and I became very close friends, and when I was in town, we would visit him at the nursing home where he was staying and make him laugh by stumbling around the room in roller blades. For someone who had so recently been bent on praying that he would wake up completely, I was amazed at how happy I was just to hear Jacob laugh.

By Christmas, Jacob could walk with assistance. The next spring he began to be able to say words. His speech was limited, but he was talking. My cousin Jacob was restored to me. He may never skateboard again, but that was not why I loved him. That was just something I loved doing with him. The fact is, I thought he was gone, I was told that he was gone; and at that point, when there was nothing left to hope for within the confines of human existence, God gave me a miracle. Not the miracle I had asked for, but a miracle nonetheless.

Another incredible gift that I only recently began to fully comprehend was the friendship I have since developed with Luke, who was eleven at the time of the accident. Luke was always the third wheel in our adventures before, but Jacob's accident left the two of us clinging to each other. We cried together and laughed together, and over the years Luke has become in many ways my favorite person in the world. The memories I have of Jacob before his accident, the trials and blessings I have experienced since Jacob's accident, and the incredible experience of having a cousin for a beyond-best friend, all are shared with Luke. Not only did God not take Jacob away, but he also gave me a wonderful friend to help me through it.

It's a beautiful work of God that Luke doesn't function as a replacement. I was never forced to forget Jacob and move on to some other best friend somewhere else in a different sphere. God had put Luke there from the beginning, right there, knowing how much I would need him.

Jacob's life now is a testimony to me of perseverance. I know sometimes it is frustrating for him to be physically limited. I don't know what that's like, but I knew Jacob before his accident, and he was never easily daunted by anything. I don't know of course, but I can imagine that many people, such as myself, if put in Jacob's position, might never have even squeezed their dad's hand in the first place. As it is, Jacob is a joy to be around. His attitude is positive, and even in his moments of greatest frustration, he is always willing to smile and look me in the eye and say, "Yeah," no matter how feeble my words of encouragement might be.

I still pray for Jacob's total recovery. As I grow older, I learn more and more that God's will is frequently different than mine; and—because my will is tainted by sin—that is a very good thing. And I don't know much about heaven, but I do believe that the saints of God will be there in their sanctified states. Fear removed, feet unshackled, Jacob and I may very well skateboard one day on streets of gold. And I'm learning that I can wait for that if I have to. Until then, I am grateful that I can talk to him. That he can still make me laugh.

God gave me twelve joyful years with Jacob. Since the accident, I have had twelve powerful, and possibly more joyful, years with Jacob. God has given me an amazing friend in Luke Damoff. God has given me a good reason to pray. Growing up in a loving, comfortable Christian home I never knew how amazingly blessed I was. Now I do. More than anything, through all of this, God has shown me what incredible blessings he has heaped on my life. Nearly every tear I cried during the summer of 1996 was really a testimony to how good God had been to me before that. And He has continued to be unduly gracious and kind to me far beyond what I could ever earn or deserve. In the only truly momentous thing that has ever happened to me, God taught me that He is faithful and that He is very good.

Philip Jones (Trinity Episcopal Church's former rector, who pulled Jacob out of the water)

On the day of Jacob's accident, we'd taken the eighth-grade kids to the lake for a canoe trip. They were playing in the water. When I joined them on the shore, people were asking about Jacob and Jeremy. Nobody knew where they were. We all called their names, but then I felt an impulse. It was as though God told me to get in the water and search. I took off my shirt and shoes. I was diving. I couldn't see anything, but I remember I dove near the bridge pilings. After a couple of dives, I felt a body. I grabbed and pulled it out.

When I got back to shore, I called, "I've got Jacob!" The kids were going crazy. I left him in the care of other adults who began CPR and then dove again to keep searching for Jeremy, but I couldn't find him. The whole thing was such a surreal experience. Like I didn't know what I'd done or why I'd done it.

Talking to the Damoffs at the hospital was very difficult for me, because we were close friends. Later that afternoon, many of the kids gathered at our house. My daughter, Cole, had been one of the students on the canoe trip. She, and many of the others who came over, had been close to Jacob. I remember talking to them—trying to help them sort out their feelings.

Four or five days later, I went to Jeremy's funeral. I was wearing so many hats . . . pastor, school representative, father. That morning it all sank in. I broke down. I called one of my best friends to pray for me.

In the days that followed, prayer seemed the thread running through everything. The whole church prayed. The entire Christian community in Marshall gathered around the Damoff family. From a pastor's perspective, this was huge. Until you're part of something like that, you don't know how the church will respond. It was amazing.

I had many great conversations with the Damoffs as they walked through this ordeal. I never saw any bitterness toward the church or the people who'd been at the lake. The insurance settlement was a no-brainer. I'm so thankful for the way it met Jacob's needs. I don't think the Damoffs knew it, but Scott Baldwin helped initiate that. He was president of Trinity's school board and a plaintiff's lawyer. We both knew it was simply what we were supposed to do.

What do you do when something like this happens? You trust God, you pray, you hold vigil. It never leaves your memory. When I see any story or movie about drowning, it takes me back, not in a horrible way, but remembering how God has worked through Jacob and the Damoffs. The miraculous improvement! The pain is still there in my memories, but it's not debilitating. It's a memory of thankfulness to God for allowing me to help as much as I did, wishing I'd been able to do more. It was a unique experience spiritually. I've gone through it. I don't talk about it much. I know it changed me. It's tucked away and God uses it.

I have so much love and respect for Jeanne and George. I admired the way they walked, prayed, and hoped—a perspective that comes from a lifelong relationship with God. Their family had an impact on many lives. It still does.

Sue Werner (Jacob's youth minister)

We all have those markers in our lives, those things that change us forever. Jacob's accident was one for me. I remember receiving the phone call and having difficulty processing what I'd heard. My thoughts vacillated from "How can he make it after being under for so long?" to "Lord, how can he not make it?"

I went straight to the hospital. People were already lining the hallways and filling the waiting room. As the youth learned of the accident, they came—one by one or in small groups. They wanted to be close. No one could have kept them away. I remember their faces: shock, concern—their eyes searching for answers—tears flowing. Everyone asked the same question: "Is Jacob going to be alright?" They wanted to do something. We all felt helpless.

The nurses allowed me to go to Jacob's bedside. I had never seen anyone with so many machines and tubes attached to him. I talked to Jacob, hoping he could hear me. I prayed aloud over him, crying out to God on his behalf.

The youth wanted to know everything, every detail of what he looked like. The next day I took my camera and snapped a picture, which I gave to Jacob's parents years later. I never showed anyone that picture until I gave it to them. It was for me. It was my connection to Jacob. I looked at the picture when I prayed for him.

Youth group was difficult for everyone for a very long time. A part of us was missing. I saw a unique bond develop among the youth. I had always thought that group of kids cared about each other, but now it intensified. The depth of caring and expressing that care for each other magnified. Everything we did, everything we planned centered around thoughts of Jacob. We made a Jacob bulletin board in the youth room, where we posted news, placed old pictures of Jacob, and so forth. It was the first thing they would check when they came into the room, to see if something new had been added. Everyone had the liberty to add to it, so there was ownership of what was placed there.

I remember the numerous times we made yellow ribbons—sometimes with other youth groups—and posted them around town. It was important for the youth to be doing something for Jacob. They wanted to make a positive, visible statement to everyone that they had not given up hope.

In addition to the ribbons, our youth group wanted to do something just for themselves that would be a constant reminder to pray for Jacob. We made "prayer bead pins." We put yellow beads onto safety pins and pinned them on our tennis shoe laces. Every time we put on our shoes we were reminded to pray. I still have mine.

When Jacob was transferred to Baylor, the kids felt disconnected. Many of them had not actually seen Jacob, but they'd known he was nearby when he was at the hospital in Marshall. Just hearing a report on him did not seem to be enough. So I took them to Baylor to see Jacob. I felt it was important that they see him, to help them feel more at peace with the situation. I don't think I ever received as much gratitude over anything else we did as I received over that trip. It confirmed to me that it was something they really needed.

Everyone changed in some way, but there were a few specific people in whom I recall seeing the greatest change. Paul Fugler was never the same again. Paul and Jacob were so much a part of each other; their thoughts and actions fed off of one another. They were inseparable and hilarious. They certainly kept things fun and interesting. Paul was lost for a long period of time. He became quiet and more of an introvert. In time he developed relationships with some of the other guys, especially Joe Chastain, but it was never the same bond that he had with Jacob.

Stephanie Hillhouse was the girl that seemed to be most affected. She was an integral part of planning the yellow ribbon events, keeping things on the Jacob Board, and so forth. Her heart was broken and aching, and it was important therapy for her to be doing something. When Jacob was in the nursing home, I don't think she missed a day of going to see him. She would go all hours of the day or night, whenever she could. She took to heart the request to help Jacob by visiting him and reading to him. She truly gave sacrificially of herself and her time.

I remember going to the nursing home, reading to Jacob, the nurses getting me to help him exercise his legs. Those are precious memories that I cherish. And I'll never forget what happened after Jacob first started saying a few words. His mom asked him if he remembered who I was. He said, "Ms. Sue." Those words were the sweetest sound to my ears! My heart leaped with joy over what God was doing in his life.

I value life—especially the lives of my children and grandchild—to such a greater degree because of Jacob. I don't think I have ever witnessed any one single incident or person that has had the effect on so many lives that Jacob has had. His life has been a miracle of God that has been so far reaching . . . further than any one of us can imagine.

On numerous occasions I have shared portions of Jacob's story. And that's just one person spreading the good news. If you multiply that by the thousands who know the story, it is mind boggling! This is what can happen when one family allows God to use them in the midst of their deep pain.

Kirk Werner (our pastor at Evangelical Presbyterian Church at the time of Jacob's accident)

I have a short list of things that have happened throughout my life—major events that bring to light what is real and what is shadow. Or perhaps another way of putting it is these events helped me to get down to what really matters. They have the capacity to sift the petty and save what is pure.

I remember getting that phone call the afternoon Jacob drowned. I was stunned, almost in a daze as I rushed to the hospital. I remember meeting George there. Praying with him as they tended to Jacob. I was powerless to do anything other than to be there with my brother who was hurting. And as uncomfortable as that may have been (uncomfortable because I had no control whatsoever over the situation) that is what I was called to do . . . just be there.

This event was a lesson for me that I am not the "answer man." I don't think people really expect answers (that doesn't mean we won't ask why), but what we need most in times such as these is to be in the Lord's presence. We are called to be His body, and a part of that is being there for one another.

Our church had lots of opportunities to do that very thing when this happened to the Damoff family. I think that strengthened us all as a church. I witnessed a great outpouring of love and concern among the church family and particularly our youth.

Something that was really special for me was my visits with Jacob in the nursing home. This was back before he could speak, but we still communicated. When he progressed to the point that he could kick a beach ball in his room, we had a great time playing "soccer." It was wonderful to see him do the things the doctors said he never would do. Granted, Jacob lost a great deal of his physical capabilities, but God has given him some precious gifts that will last forever. Gifts that are special and tailored just for Jacob.

I still don't know why God allows some things to happen. And that's OK . . . more than OK. That is the way it should be, because God is God and I am not! I love the analogy of the woven tapestry. Our perspective is from the back of the extensive needlework. All we see is a gnarled mess of threads. But God's perspective is from the front, which displays a beautiful work of art.

Faith is trusting God in all things. He has promised us that He will always be with us. If we learn through these hard times, we will know that His presence is enough. I have found that I can make do without a lot of things. But the sole necessity of life is His presence.

I feel woefully inadequate to try to communicate the full impact all of this has had on me, my family, and my ministry. In closing, I do want to say it has deepened my appreciation for each new day and encouraged me to treasure the close relationships God has given me, even those that transcend time and space.

Mary Carlile, M.D. (the head of Jacob's medical team at Baylor Institute of Rehabilitation)

I remember very distinctly how ill Jacob was when he came to us. He showed signs of sepsis (systemic infection), and due to the close proximity of the sinuses to the brain, I was sure that meningitis was the next phase we would face. I called in other specialists—an infectious disease specialist, an ear nose and throat specialist, and most importantly a pediatric neurologist to assist in Jacob's care and to help me give the Damoffs a realistic prognosis for his survival. I remember trying to gently prepare them for what we all thought was inevitable—his death.

Most vividly, I remember the response of Jeanne and George. They were grief stricken, but completely able to put Jacob's life in God's hands. They were willing to give him up if that was His will. I remember Jeanne's telling me of a worship service they attended in Dallas during which tears were streaming down her face, but the strength of her faith never left her.

During times of crisis and life-threatening illness, it is common for people to seek God and invoke His help. Usually, it is "Lord, let Thy will be done, but let it be the following. . . ." To most, their faith is only for a positive outcome. Instead of hollow "God talk" as my chaplain calls it, it was obvious to Jacob's treatment team that the Damoffs were the "real McCoy." While tragic, it was uplifting to see how completely and utterly they trusted that the ordained outcome would be for the best.

Jacob struck everyone who saw him at BIR as an angel-like figure. He appeared beautiful and fragile at that time. He gradually but definitively "turned the corner" as one serious complication after another was faced and overcome. By the time he left us, he was even showing some early responses to his favorites—his family.

I know the Damoffs continued to have many more difficult months and years, and I credit their commitment and love with the triumph Jacob has achieved. Never, however, in my wildest dreams did I think he would improve to his current functional status. When he walked off the elevator at our hospital many months later for a visit, our staff was overwhelmed. We are accustomed to seeing people improve, but we considered the recovery we had witnessed in Jacob a true miracle.

To this day, I refer to Jacob's story when I'm speaking to families about the limitations of doctors and the medical world in being able to predict recovery or demise. We do our best to use the knowledge and scientific treatments we have to foster recovery, but the final result is truly not in our hands. I believe that sharing Jacob's story with other families allows them to hold on to hope.

"Jacob's Song" has also been a blessing to the staff, families, and patients at BIR and beyond. Debbie Boatright-Camacho came and sang it to our patients. It struck a common emotional chord in those suffering from all nature of disabilities. In my own life, my mother has been bedfast for the past five years due to multiple sclerosis. A strong Christian, she has been courageous as her life has taken on very small dimensions. She has some depression; however, when she feels the sadness overtaking her, she plays "Jacob's Song" and is able to let go of the burdens. His story inspires her to turn it over to the Lord and place it in His hands. We leave the CD in the player at all times.

In summary, those of us who were fortunate to know Jacob at BIR will never forget him. He continues to be an example of hope to patients and families undergoing critical injuries and illness. His life has been a shining example to our staff.

Debbie Boatright-Camacho (former student at ETBU and composer of "Jacob's Song")

Arriving home after an exhausting day at the university, I found myself in a rather less-than-chipper mood. Our house was in great need of attention, assignments were due, and I had completely run out of clean clothes to wear. I dropped about thirty pounds of books on the floor, fell to my knees, and began an attempt at a weary prayer. "God, I'm tired—family, church, school, my music, our home—I need help."

Before I could release the words, the thought of Jacob and his family entered my mind. Quickly, my petty whines turned to brokenness. Tears filled my eyes as I thought about the pain that he and his family must be going through. How insignificant my problems became as an abundant amount of compassion overwhelmed my heart.

As tears fell, I began to whisper out a prayer. I stumbled over the words to present to God. Almost at the mention of Jacob's name, lyrics began to fill my mind. I ripped out a page from a class notebook, grabbed my guitar, and began to play and write. It seemed as though the music just appeared behind the lyrics—like heaven had already written *this* song. Rarely do I experience such infinite stillness and internal isolation when composing. It felt as if the world halted momentarily that I might receive clearly the perfect words. "Jacob's Song" was truly a divine gift.

Via the "Visions of Love" CD, the song has literally traveled all over the world. I have been told that it was even translated into Russian. A missionary there returned to tell me that many had been blessed by the message in the song. I've lost count of the comments and letters I've received with similar regards.

A short time after sharing the song with the family, Jeanne began to tell me about a prayer she prayed for those who prayed for Jacob. For all those who mentioned Jacob's name to God, she asked that God would simply "meet them wherever they are." How amazingly unselfish and humanly uncharacteristic for a family to desire that God would use their pain as an opportunity for Him to touch others' lives! I know, with no uncertainty, that when I mentioned Jacob's name to God, the heavens opened up and He met me right there on my knees . . . with "Jacob's Song."

Amy Barron Pecory (ETBU student who lived with the Damoffs in 1997)

I was in Mr. Damoff's office when he received a phone call that Jacob had been in an accident. I remember the look on his face and the bad feeling I got in my stomach. I could tell the accident was serious. Things began happening so fast. The exam I had taken that day was forgotten, along with the other petty things we were discussing.

I went to the hospital. I saw Jeanne as she arrived, and I remember the concern in her eyes. Being a mother, I can't imagine what she was thinking. I watched the two parents embrace and begin to pray for Jacob. I remember that struck me as incredible. I know we are taught to take our burdens to God, but their faith seemed like such a foreign thing to me at that moment.

I was so consumed by my feelings that I hadn't thought to pray. I left the hospital not knowing Jacob's accident would have a profound effect on my life. I believe that was the beginning of an incredible time of learning for me. Over the course of the next few months, I witnessed a family show amazing strength. I learned that the Damoffs truly gave their burdens to the Lord. They showed me that in Him we can face any of life's hurdles. Without Him we cannot survive.

I witnessed family and friends praying at all times. But I also witnessed their lives. I noticed they weren't just prayerful, they were faithful. I have experienced tragedy in my life before, and never have I seen people more committed to accepting God's will for their lives. I am sure there were times of doubt, especially when Jacob was in Dallas at Baylor. But I was comforted by the clarity of their faith.

On numerous occasions I heard Mr. Damoff share his faith with other families in crisis. Although I don't know the outcomes of those conversations, I believe it was significant that he was able to share Christ's love and comfort with others while his child was so incredibly ill. That not only challenged me to be more open about my faith, but it challenged my faith. Would I be able to allow God to work through me if a loved one were so desperately ill? Where did my faith lie? I am a student of science. If I know that the brain can only withstand so much trauma, can I believe with my mind and my spirit that God can heal such a person?

I struggled during those months with my lack of faith. I spent a lot of time evaluating what I believed and to what extent. I was building a foundation for my faith that has been relevant to my growth as a Christian. Though I was not raised in a home where Scripture was taught, I began to search the Word for instances where God fulfilled His promises.

I found promises that applied to Jacob's situation. Although I had heard these words before, they didn't become "real" until this point in my walk with Christ: "Do not let your hearts be troubled. Trust in God; trust also in me" (John 14:1 NIV), and "I will never leave you nor forsake you" (Josh. 1:5 NIV).

Jacob continued to teach me about perseverance through hardship as he improved while staying in the nursing facility in Marshall. I had the opportunity of participating in his therapy. I spent time reading to him and rubbing his arms and legs with textured gloves. Each day held new challenges for Jacob. His passion to overcome motivated me to have a passion in my life as well. Because of Jacob, I do not take my days for granted. I realize all the blessings God has given me today might be gone tomorrow. When you realize how brief our time on earth is, you become acutely aware of our purpose here. I began to understand that God had a specific plan for my life and I needed to pursue it with the same passion that Jacob was pursuing his recovery.

During the time I lived with the Damoff family I learned more than I could possibly put into words. I had the unique experience of seeing Jacob's progress and the wonderful little things that happened to keep his family and me encouraged about his possibilities.

Jacob definitely has a strong will. I remember at one point we thought his progress had hit a plateau. He was jumping on the trampoline with

Mr. Damoff. We were all standing around watching him laugh. For me, it was just wonderful to see Jacob smile again and to know that he was enjoying himself.

When they took a break from jumping, I said, "Jacob, if you want to jump some more, say 'Mom.'" He looked at Mrs. Damoff and spoke. I don't think he had said anything since his accident. It was a defining moment for me. God gives us little tidbits of His incredible love for us when we least suspect it. God gave me a sneak peek at what He would accomplish. That is when I knew with God *all* things are possible. Not just the things we think should be or could be possible, but all things.

It is an amazing moment in your life when you realize that the Lord is in your presence. He watches over all that goes on, and when you least expect it, He gives you a beautiful sunset or a refreshing shower or a few words from a boy who hasn't spoken in a year. He is full of surprises. That is such an incredible thing to realize. I continued to be amazed by God's power over Jacob's circumstances. He was able to learn to swallow, eat, walk, and talk again.

As I said, I learned so many things while living with the Damoffs. Each member of their family was able to teach and influence me each day I lived with them. I felt like a sponge soaking up all of the godly wisdom that this family shared with me. If I had to narrow it down to one truth that I took from that experience, I guess it would be that God is in control.

He is in control of our circumstances when we submit to Him and when we choose to try to handle things on our own. The only difference is the outcome. I was able to witness a family wholly submit to God's will for their lives. It is an incredible act of obedience that I attempt to mimic each day. I was able to witness a family rejoicing in God's infinite power, even in the face of such a terrible tragedy. I was able to witness a boy defy many limitations that modern medicine claimed he would never overcome. I witnessed faith that was childlike and submissive to God's control. I witnessed a family truly living in faith. And it is a lifestyle that I continue to strive for each day of my life.

Joanna Blackwelder (mother of Jake, the boy who drowned one year after Jacob)

Thinking about how God used Jacob and the Damoff family in our lives, the one thing that keeps coming to mind is hope. I remember so clearly how confused Mark and I were after Jake's accident. We had so many questions about coma. What level would Jake come out of it? What would this injury mean to Jake's quality of life? How would this affect the other children? What would be the best way Mark and I could help Jake?

I remember specifically asking George and Jeanne many of these questions, knowing now, of course, they didn't have the answers. But what they did share with us were their experiences with Jacob, their faith that God would see them through, and an assurance that, where there is love, there is joy and happiness no matter the circumstance.

Mark and I left there with hope. The Damoff family was God's tool to show us that no matter how many unknowns there are, no matter how many questions left unanswered, God will provide a way for a family that loves Him and loves each other.

And I remember something else equally important. I remember meeting Jacob, seeing his smiling face, and thinking, *God, if my son can have that same joy that is living in Jacob, then I know it will be alright.*

Our sons' accidents were just a year apart, on the same day and so similar in nature that I still get chills thinking about it. Jacob was doing so well that he didn't need his wheelchair anymore, and it had his name—my son's name—on the seat. All those little things were God's provision of hope. Yes, Mark and I left there feeling not so alone and with a renewed hope God would walk with us through all the uncharted territory just as He was doing with the Damoff family. I don't think Mark and I ever thanked the Damoffs properly for that visit. I offer our gratitude now.

Rusty Mauldin (Jacob's aide since 1997)

Working with Jacob has changed my whole outlook. Everything has more meaning. Being around the Damoffs is like being around angels. I've learned more in the past ten years than in the twenty previous ones.

Now I know life is about people and taking care of them. It's not about what I want.

God was not important to me before. I was wrapped up in material things. Then I saw the Damoffs' lifestyle, and that's how I wanted to be. I needed to change mentally, to focus less on the material and more on spiritual matters. It's not about what I have.

Before their influence, I worried about my appearance. I wanted to show off—impress people with external things. Now I don't care about that. Before, I worried about clothes, hair, what I drove. I was worldly. I realize now how shallow I was. Now I'm focused on responsibility. Before, I wanted to turn heads. Now I couldn't care less about that. I care about what God wants me to do and think about.

Working with Jacob changed my whole attitude. Even with all their problems, the Damoffs were "carefree." They worked together as a team. Watching them, I learned to share and work with others. I've learned that it's better to be in unity, to work with those in your life. Before, I'd get mad at my wife and kids and refuse to work things out. Now I work through things with them. I see what's truly important. I got that from watching the Damoffs.

The other day my uncle said, "Girls are nothing but trouble." It made me mad. And I thought, "It's not true. Look at Grace." It's how you raise them—the way you interact with your children. I'm learning not to worry about my children, because I see the Damoffs trusting God even after this happened. I want to be involved in my kids' lives. I've seen how relationships can work. I've seen the values that I want lived out in the Damoffs.

I can honestly say, working with Jacob has changed my whole life. Before coming to work for the Damoffs, I'd always been short on patience and quick tempered. With Jacob, I had to try to understand. I had to have patience to make my job work, and I soon realized I needed it in other areas of my life as well. I see a difference in how I relate to my family. I realized I *wanted* to be patient, because I cared about Jacob and his family. I've learned to carry that into all my relationships. I don't take things for granted anymore. Now I know each day is a gift. Anything can happen, so I appreciate the people and the good things in my life.

Working with Jacob has shown me I want to help people. I've become a "people person." As hard-headed as Jacob is, being able to accomplish things with him has taught me I can have influence. I now realize I want to be a teacher, to help others as I've helped Jacob.

The Damoffs have taught me to remain positive—not to give up. Sometimes I worry, but I realize that, if something bad happens, you can work though it. Every day when I wake up, I look for the good in whatever circumstances I'm in. When bad things happen, I know there's good somewhere. I always look for the positive. There's Something beyond me. It's easy to lose focus, but when you feel Someone helping you through, you get back on track. I've watched God carry the Damoffs through. I know He will carry me, too.

Allan Thompson (interim pastor at Evangelical Presbyterian Church for a ten-month period in 1999 and 2000)

I was the interim pastor at Jacob's church for a period of ten months. As a friend of the Damoff family, I had known the children for a number of years, and my sons had formed friendships with them as well. I was there at the hospital the day Jacob was brought in from the drowning, both to pray for the family and to encourage the fledgling rector of Trinity Episcopal Church, Philip Jones. Many of the area clergy were also there that day.

I say that as background for this incident. After accepting the position of interim pastor, I was privileged to lead out in my first Communion time with the congregation. In this church the elders stood behind prayer railings that lined the stage and administered the elements to those who came forward and kneeled. The pastor stood behind the central altar, and usually the ones who came to him were those who either could not kneel or needed special assistance.

I had served a few of the older members when I saw Jacob coming up to the altar. I wondered what needs he would have, but I saw his sister accompanying him and hoped she would take the lead. Jacob could grasp the bread and the cup but needed someone to help him get the juice to his mouth without spilling it.

I watched with mild interest until the name of his sister came to mind—Grace.

Then I thought, *Grace is enabling a child of God to enjoy the presence of God when he could not in his own strength.* I ceased to watch with interest and realized I was having a sermon acted out in front of my eyes. It was a deep revelation to me of what grace has been in my life, and it has stayed with me as one of the greatest single moments of worship I have ever experienced.

Since that time I have rejoiced with the family in watching Jacob progress in many ways. He is a remarkable young man whom God continues to use as a witness to many of His love . . . and His grace.

Mary Jones (long-time member of Evangelical Presbyterian Church)

Had it been up to us, I am sure none of us would have chosen the events that involved Jacob some years ago. But God in His wisdom and love saw the beauty that would unfold from what we all considered a tragedy at the time. Because we know God's ways are not our ways, we can accept what happened to Jacob and find good in it.

The subsequent metamorphosis that has taken place in Jacob has been awesome to all of us who have watched. Witnessing his emergence from the cocoon of death, waiting as his wings dried, and then watching him fly into the wind has been a beautiful thing. As Jacob tries those wings of independence and trust, our hearts are warmed by his quick smile and winsome personality, his lifting of his hands in praise, and his courage and successes.

I sometimes wonder, *What would our part of the body be like without Jacob just as he is?* I am afraid we would not be as forgiving and accepting. We wouldn't desire to be more like the Jesus we see in Jacob.

It is hard to put into words all that Jacob's ordeal has done to bring encouragement, hope, and the grace and love of the sovereign God into our hearts. It is wonderful to know God loves us with such an incomprehensible love that He will not permit anything to come into our lives that He doesn't want to use for our good and His glory. We all probably have had questions why this accident would have happened to a vibrant, Christian young man. In retrospect I feel it was, in part, to mold, refine, and shape us more into the image of Christ as we united our hearts and prayers of faith for Jacob.

Being part of Jacob's experience has given me a lot for which to be thankful. I've seen God's grace played out in each member of the Damoff family. I've seen Jacob's transformation from an ordinary teen to an extraordinary young man whose relationship with Jesus is enviable. I've seen God's continued provision, day by day, for all the unique needs the Damoff family has faced. And I've witnessed Jacob's metamorphosis, which gives hope to many and makes our lives much richer. God is faithful.

Natalie Dowd Grubbs (Jacob's best friend)

Before Jacob's accident, I leaned on him in so many ways. He was my best friend, and the person I went to for advice on any topic. Although years ago now, I still remember writing in my journal: "Jacob will not always be here. I must put my trust in the Lord."

Though that specific entry dealt more with Jacob's plans to leave our private school and attend public after ninth grade, the truth applied to every circumstance in my life. I had to choose to trust the Lord in everything. Not long after I wrote that entry, Jacob drowned.

Losing Jacob made me want to protect everyone I loved. I wanted to keep them in my sight. I wanted to control events to prevent anything bad from happening to them. I wanted to take care of them.

I decided to be a nurse because of what I went through with Jacob. It was the caring for people—not the science—that drew me. I wanted to be the kind of nurse who reaches out to everyone involved in tragedy. I don't remember any nurses asking me how *I* was handling the tragedy that struck my best friend. I decided to become that nurse.

I work in labor and delivery, and the other night I was talking with one of my patients. She shared with me that she had lost her first baby. After having her second child, she'd had a hard time allowing her daughter to do anything on her own.

I understood her tendencies more than I wanted to. I told her about my own desire to control things because my experience with Jacob hurt so badly. But then I began telling her all the amazing things God did in and through Jacob, and I realized I don't need to try to be in control. I don't even want to be in control. Whatever God does will be good. As I encouraged this woman to trust God with her daughter, I realized I needed to do the same with the people in my life.

What God continues to show me is that He is sovereign. It wasn't until recently that I realized what that meant. My alarm clock doesn't wake me up in the morning. God does. Gravity doesn't pull me back to the earth, but rather the Lord. I have been taught so much science that I sometimes forget the truth I base my life upon.

I cannot control one thing. I realize I am not promised my husband forever, a comfortable life, or healthy children. Even after such a profound experience of God's mercy years ago, I still desire to control my life. But I'm learning more and more that God is sovereign. Nothing will ever happen outside His loving plan.

I now have a sweet child of my own, Lawson Jacob (after Jacob, of course). Often as I am rocking him at night, I think of Jacob and his mother. As I hold him, I do not know his future. And I am thankful. The pain that might lie ahead would be unbearable. But what I have learned is to trust God with open hands. Lawson is given to me as a gift to care for, but not to idolize. I must hold on loosely, and yet while doing so, I have also learned to cherish every moment that he is with me in this life.

I'll never forget Jacob. My memories will never be erased. Now, all these years later, I still think of Jacob often and pray for his continued healing. And I trust God that all things will work for good in his life and in mine.

George Damoff (Jacob's father)

"My God, my God, why have You forsaken me?" (Ps. 22:1).

Psalm 22 is a mysterious and miraculous poem. It prophetically reveals, in intimate detail, the anguish of God the Son as He struggles against faithless forces in the world. It seemed that God the Father had forsaken Him, that His audible groans were unheard, and that His hope for a good, productive life would be futile. The depths of sorrow recorded in the psalm, however, are superseded by the ultimate triumph of His strength over the circumstance of His cruel, yet redemptive, death.

The strength of rushing water dislodges anything that lacks a strong, steadfast anchor. Jacob's near drowning on the afternoon of May 23, 1996 was a catastrophic deluge that inundated my faith in a good Creator. Yet, by the kind intention of God, He desired to reveal in a most intimate manner that He is Strength greater than all earthly powers—that He is, indeed, *my* Strength.

The day when Jacob, against his will, was pulled down into the murky water, I was pulled, against my will, into a turbulent struggle against hopelessness and despair. Overwhelmed by my wrestling with this raging current, I scarcely could see the struggles of the rest of my family (Jeanne, Grace, and Luke)—let alone attempt to help them. Even so, God, in kindness, covered my many weaknesses and met their needs.

From the moment I received that first phone call from the Trinity Episcopal secretary, life became a paradox. My survival depended on trust in God, yet He was the very One who had allowed this horrible event to occur. Do all believers who seek to find meaning in their suffering wrestle with this irony? Does the confusion caused by this paradox lead many to a bitterness of soul, a pursuit of understanding that leaves them gasping for air? Is it through this mystery that our Creator chooses to draw us into a greater experience of His grace?

Confronted with cruel circumstances, at first I had to choose to trust God from one minute to the next. Over time I learned to abide in trust for hours, days, weeks, and months. Pain and sorrow thrust me on my God. My Redeemer became my Strength.

Jacob has been miraculously raised from the dead. Although the scars of this turmoil are still evident, the cruel waters mysteriously transformed my son into a redemptive blessing for many. Who am I to resist the ways of God the Father with His children? I yield to God the Holy Spirit to guide my thoughts in order to understand His purposes that allow evil, destructive events. I choose to follow the Son of God through a world that is antagonistic to the faith that leads to life—the faith that enables me to trust in a good Creator.

As God the Son trusted His Father in Psalm 22, so I trust that the LORD God has intended goodness to emerge from the waters that *almost* destroyed Jacob, as well as me and my family. The LORD God is near us. He hears prayers weakly whispered from pain and sorrow, and by His strength He takes the fragile hope of those who trust Him and transforms it into good, productive lives.

> I will tell of Your name to my brethren;
> In the midst of the assembly I will praise You.
> You who fear the LORD, praise Him;
> All you descendants of Jacob, glorify Him,
> And stand in awe of Him, all you descendants of Israel.
> For He has not despised nor abhorred the affliction of the afflicted;
> Nor has He hidden His face from him;
> But when he cried to Him for help, He heard.
>
> (Ps. 22:22–24)

APPENDIX B:

Q & A: GOD'S PURPOSES IN SUFFERING

Who are you, O man, who answers back to God? The thing molded will not say to the molder, "Why did you make me like this," will it?

—Rom. 9:20

Common questions arise when Christians face acute suffering in their own lives or the lives of those they love. I believe the Bible provides reliable evidence of God's sovereign purposes in suffering. Though I don't hold myself up as an expert theologian, and I certainly don't claim to have all the answers, my search for understanding has led me to a place of peace and freedom. In this section I hope to share those insights in a conversational manner, accessible to anyone regardless of prior scriptural knowledge.

Q: Does a loving God foreordain tragic events?

A: Let's consider a few biblical examples. Genesis 15 records a series of promises God made to Abram. The first was, "Do not fear, Abram, I am a shield to you; your reward shall be very great" (verse 1). That's a promise anyone would be thrilled to receive. Next God declared He would give Abram an heir from his own body, and his descendants would be as numerous as the stars (verses 4–5). Also wonderful. Then God promised Abram the land that would become Israel (verse 7). This just gets better and better. But God wasn't finished. Abram fell into a deep sleep, and God came to him with another promise.

"Know for certain that your descendants will be strangers in a land that is not theirs, where they will be enslaved and oppressed four hundred years. But I will also judge the nation whom they will serve, and afterward they will come out with many possessions" (verses 13–14).

What? Was God saying many of Abram's descendants would be born and die in slavery and oppression? Not exactly the kind of promise one wants to hear.

And yet, God ordained it to be so, and it was so. Four generations of God's chosen people lived and died enslaved in Egypt. They suffered humiliation and abuse. They were beaten and deprived. Pharaoh forced them to toss their newborn sons into the Nile. God knew about it all in advance. And He didn't prevent it.

Did God love those people? Did He take note of their pain? Were the hairs of their heads numbered? Yes. And God fulfilled His divine purposes through Abram and his descendants.

We have no record or knowledge of the way God worked in individual hearts and lives during those four hundred difficult years. But we know their suffering was a necessary part of God's plan.

The life of Joseph illustrates this truth as well. Chapters 37 through 45 of Genesis unfold the story. Though Joseph was his father's favorite, and God gave him dreams that seemed to promise future greatness, his life went from bad to worse. His jealous brothers plotted to murder him, then sold him to Midianite traders instead. He gained favor as a slave in Egypt, until his owner's wife tried to seduce him and then falsely accused him of attacking her. Unjustly imprisoned, he served his fellow prisoners, but his kindness was forgotten, and he languished for years. Joseph suffered thirteen years of persecution, when his worst crimes were being a spoiled brat and bragging about his dreams.

Through it all, God humbled Joseph's heart and strengthened his faith, preparing him to take a position of great authority. Joseph ultimately preserved millions from starvation, including his own family. When Joseph revealed himself to his brothers, he said, "Do not be grieved or angry with yourselves, because you sold me here, for God sent me before you to preserve life . . . Now, therefore, it was not you who sent me here, but God" (45:5, 8).

Seventeen years later, when their father died, Joseph's brothers again feared punishment for their crimes against him, but Joseph said, "Do not be afraid, for am I in God's place? And as for you, you meant evil against me, but God meant it for good" (Gen. 50:19–20).

Joseph harbored no bitterness about a plan that led him through years of suffering. He understood God's greater purpose.

Of course, someone might argue that Abram and Joseph dealt with the God of the Old Testament, sometimes portrayed as a wrathful God of judgment. When Jesus came, didn't He usher in a new age of grace and favor with God? Doesn't this mean our struggles with pain and sorrow should be over?

It would be nice to think that the "mean" God who ordained suffering in the past reinvented Himself as a kinder, gentler model after Christ's sacrifice for sin. But we would have to throw out large portions of the New Testament to embrace that belief.

After Paul's Damascus road encounter with Christ in Acts 9, God sent Ananias to restore Paul's sight. God said, "Go, for he is a chosen instrument of Mine, to bear My name before the Gentiles and kings and the sons of Israel; for I will show him how much he must suffer for My name's sake" (verses 15–16).

Imagine an altar call along those lines: "You're invited to come and receive Christ and see how much you must suffer for His name's sake. Please form a single line, and no shoving." And yet, Paul had encountered Jesus, and there was no turning back. Second Corinthians 11:23–28 details a few of the hardships Paul endured for Christ. He persevered with joy, because he had learned to fix his eyes on Jesus. God called Paul to suffer, and few have made contributions to God's kingdom as significant as Paul's.

One might think, "OK, that's all fine and good. But Paul was an apostle, and I am just your average Christian, trying to live a good life and get by. I love the Lord. I read the Bible. I tithe to my church. Is it too much to expect God to bless me in return? Hasn't He promised me abundant life?"

He has indeed. But I wonder if God defines "abundant" the same way we like to. We ask God to make our circumstances pleasant, and to please do it now. God is working on hearts, and that takes time. A lifetime.

Our best example is Jesus. God foreordained Christ's suffering before the foundation of the world, because He knew Jesus would be the only perfect sacrifice for sin. According to Hebrews 5:8, Jesus suffered during His earthly life to learn obedience. After all, "no servant is greater than his master" (John 13:16 NIV). If God used suffering to train His Son, should we expect to be perfected through pampering and ease?

A big part of understanding why God ordains suffering lies in trying to see from God's perspective. What we call bad, God may know to be good. We can trust God to accomplish His eternal plans with perfect faithfulness (Isa. 46:9–10). We find peace when we learn to trust His wisdom.

Q: If God is all-powerful, why doesn't He just make everything perfect? Doesn't He want us to be happy?

A: Some Christians claim that God does not ordain tragic events. They declare God's will is for everyone to be happy, healthy, and prosperous. Doctrine along this line is popular because it focuses on the fulfillment of human comforts and desires.

Though this teaching sounds appealing on the surface, if carried to its logical conclusion, a frightening reality emerges: There is no power sufficient to overcome evil. If God had the power to bring "His will" (i.e., universal health and wealth) to pass, terrible things wouldn't be happening in the world. Therefore, God must not be sovereign. He must not be enthroned in the heavens, far above all rule, authority, might and dominion, as Ephesians 1:20–21 states. He must not be doing according to His will in the armies of heaven and among the inhabitants of the earth, as Nebuchadnezzar recognized and proclaimed in Daniel 4:35.

If happiness is the pinnacle of existence, then one must conclude God is impotent, not omnipotent. After all, doesn't it follow that if He were all-powerful, He would accomplish His will? And isn't His will for me to be happy and to have what I want?

God *is* all-powerful and all-wise, and He loves us too much to give us what we think we want. God uses suffering to teach us endurance and to perfect our character. "Consider it all joy, my brethren, when you encounter various trials, knowing that the testing of your faith produces endurance. And let endurance have its perfect result, so that you may be perfect and complete, lacking in nothing" (Jas. 1:2–4). My idea of "perfect" and God's idea may be two entirely different things.

God created humankind for *His* pleasure and glory. Rather than being offended by the difficulties we encounter, we should stand amazed that He fills our lives with innumerable blessings, none of which we could ever begin to merit. What a marvel! God, who is worthy of all glory and praise, chooses to lavish His goodness on me, when all I deserve is the wages of my sin: death and separation from Him.

And yet, God created me with feelings and desires. Does God love *only* His glory? Doesn't He love me, too? The wonderful truth is He does! The cross is the measure of His love. Jesus came to redeem us from sin and self, and we are made righteous in Him, fit to enter into God's presence.

God is preparing believers to reign with Him in eternity (Rev. 3:21). The church will be Jesus' spotless bride, as awesome as an army with banners (Eph. 5:27; Song of Sol. 6:4), and she won't become that way through self-indulgence.

We love to claim God's magnificent promises, but before we can begin to comprehend them, we must overcome an earthbound point of view. God uses suffering to purify His Son's bride. As we trust God through trials, our faith grows. Faith is more precious than gold (1 Pet. 1:7), and certainly more precious than any material blessing or physical comfort I may desire.

Q: I'm not a very strong person. Since God gives us only what we can handle, doesn't that mean He won't bring tragedy into my life?

A: God's personal involvement with people is a beautiful mystery. He knows us better than we know ourselves. He knows our thoughts, and His thoughts toward us outnumber the sand (Ps. 139:17–18). God knows the number of hairs on each head (Luke 12:7). He takes note of every tear shed (Ps. 56:8). He prepares our path, and He goes before us to remove obstacles (Isa. 42:16). He also goes with us as our shield, and behind us to guard us (Deut. 31:8; Isa. 52:12). He covers us with the shadow of His wings (Ps. 36:7; 57:1). He hides us in the secret place of the Most High (91:1). He guards our going out and coming in (121:8). He loves us so much that He became flesh, experienced human pain and temptation, and took our place in death. His deep love and tender intimacy defy explanation.

And yet, in many circumstances He appears unkind. We gladly recognize the Lord's hand in blessing, but when He places us in painful or difficult circumstances, we become confused. Though the Bible cites numerous examples of God's people enduring hardship by His design, we shrink from the possibility that our own path may lead into a dark valley.

No healthy person desires to suffer. It's not fun. We pray for provision and protection, and then we trust God to answer our prayers. I believe God is pleased when we live joyful lives, thanking Him for every great and simple pleasure. He is our loving Father, and He wants us to feel protected and safe.

But many Christians live with a false sense of security. We expect God to prevent *any* disaster from overtaking us. Even though we know tragic events occur every day, humans are by nature egocentric, operating under the naïve assumption that "God will not let it happen to me."

Before I had children, whenever I'd encounter a parent or caregiver with a disabled child, I thought, *God would never give me a child like that, because He knows I couldn't handle it.* I expected God to spare me from certain trials based on my natural weakness.

Such perspective denies the nature of grace. God gives grace when it is needed. He gives wisdom for actual difficulties we face. We can't imagine ourselves overcoming tragedy, because hypothetical grace and wisdom can't compare with the realities God imparts when real needs arise.

God's wisdom determines our path, and He doesn't consult our predispositions for suggestions. When we don't see how we'll survive, He plants our feet on a solid rock and holds us there. As we stand on that rock—Jesus Christ—unmoved by even the strongest winds and waves, we experience a blessing beyond description. In a way that can only be revealed in the midst of suffering, we know His grace.

God *does* give us only what we can handle. But He knows we can do all things through Him (Phil. 4:13).

Q. If God is loving and sovereign, how do you explain all the unspeakable horrors that happen in the world?

A. History reveals account after account of horrific suffering: war, disease, genocide, tyranny, and terrorism. In every generation, evil has touched individuals, families, communities, and whole nations. Unbelievers scoff, "If there really is a God, where is He? How could a loving God stand by while evil prevails?"

Many conclude that, if there is a God, He is callous and indifferent to pain. As Christians we grope for answers, yearning to reconcile the suffering we see in the world—and even in our own lives—with what we believe about God.

Pain tends to make people introspective. The incessant throbbing shoves other thoughts aside. Self-pity is a cage trapping pain's captives and keeping them from understanding God's plans. Yet, there is always a grand design. *I* am not the center of the universe. God and His purposes are.

God acts for His name's sake (Ezek. 36:22–23). The ultimate motive behind all He does is His own glory. His thoughts are higher than ours; His ways are past finding out (Isa. 55:9). He is enthroned in the heavens. We are on earth, His footstool (66:1). We were created by Him and for Him (Col. 1:16); some of us He exalts, while others He brings low (1 Sam. 2:7).

Psalm 139:16 confirms that before my son Jacob was born, every day was ordained for him and foreknown by God. God knew Jacob would "pass through the waters." True, this isn't the path I would have chosen. But who am I to question God? Can the pot say to the Potter, "Why did You make me this way?" (Rom. 9:20). "Why did You mold my son for fifteen years into a beautiful vessel, then mar Your own handiwork and strike him down?"

As hard as it may have been for me to see the good or the sense in this, I could nevertheless accept that God is responsible for His own glory, and He doesn't need or ask for my opinions on how to best accomplish it. However, He does offer me mercy and comfort in my pain. He gives me the strength to handle what His wisdom chooses for me.

Peace comes from trusting God, even when I can't understand His ways. When I cry out to Him in my sorrow, He draws near. Faith lifts me above temporal desires and expectations, and I catch glimpses of the eternal. When I encounter suffering I didn't think I could handle—the thing I dreaded most—it presses me into prayer, where I'm conformed to the image of Christ.

"And we know that God causes all things to work together for good to those who love God, to those who are called according to His purpose" (Rom. 8:28). *All* things. I once heard a preacher say, "All means all, and that's all 'all' means." We won't always be able to see what God is accomplishing, but we can trust He is working for good in His people's lives, even when it appears that evil has prevailed. Such faith is precious to God and powerful beyond our comprehension.

Q: I would think God's blessings would reflect His glory to the world. How does suffering bring glory to God?

A: Let's consider Job. Job was a wealthy, God-honoring man. Why would God give Satan permission to wipe him out? No flippant decision precipitated God's allowing Satan to destroy Job's family, possessions, and health. God exploited Satan's pride, using him as a tool for furthering God's will in Job's life and preparing Job for eternity.

Before his affliction, Job was a righteous man. But he lacked a true revelation of the holy God he served (Job 42:5). When Job's friends encouraged him to confess his sins, he maintained his innocence. Though he clung to faith, he also clung to belief in his own integrity (Job 31).

The events in Job's life were not the result of a casual wager between Satan and God. A loving Father was chastening His son (Job 38–41). Compared to other men, Job was a prime specimen of faith and goodness. But he had spiritual pride. In the intense fires of suffering, the dross rises to the surface, where God can skim it off and make us pure.

In the end, Job's life and attitude brought more glory to God than he had been able to do as a self-righteous man inundated with blessings.

Job's godliness reflected holy reverence and dependence. He became a man fit to stand in God's presence (Job 42).

Here's a more contemporary example. When I was a freshman at Stephen F. Austin State University, my pastor's wife, Mrs. Dodson, introduced me to Amy Carmichael's writings. During college and as a young bride, I read as many of her books as I could get my hands on. God used her to mold my faith.

Amy was an Englishwoman who went to the mission field just before the dawn of the twentieth century. She began her ministry as a young woman, and she remained a single missionary for the rest of her life.

Though Amy first served in Japan, God moved her to India, where she discovered the underground practice of trafficking young girls into temple prostitution. Poverty-stricken parents, induced by Hindu priests to sell their young daughters into "temple service," delivered innocent children into a system of depravity and perverse abuse. "Married to the god," the children existed to satisfy the carnal pleasure of so-called worshippers.

Amy spent the rest of her life rescuing girls from this fate and raising them in an orphanage she founded. In her middle age, she was inspecting a building project and, in the twilight, failed to see a hole that had been dug in the wrong spot. She fell, injuring her leg. Though not severe by current medical standards, the injury was not properly treated and resulted in a life of constant pain and invalidism.

Amy wrote of this experience and her struggle to come to grips with why God had allowed it. Her final analysis was this: There are no "second causes." God is in control, and the events that happen in our lives must therefore be His will.

Though most Christians would admire Amy's willingness to submit to God even in extreme pain, many might wonder why God would ordain a path of suffering for her. Amy had devoted her life to God's service. Why wouldn't God choose to bless her with good health and long life?

During this period of suffering in Amy's life she wrote most of her books and poetry. Her impact on Christians who have read her works cannot be overstated. Elisabeth Elliot, a respected missionary, author, and speaker, wrote Amy's biography. In the preface of *A Chance to Die,* she explains, "Amy Carmichael became for me what some now call a role model. She was far more than that. She was my first spiritual mother. She showed me the shape of godliness."

God removed Amy from active ministry and gave her a new calling: intercession and writing. As a result, the world is a richer place. But why did God use a painful, debilitating illness to accomplish His purpose? Why is suffering so often God's chosen tool? Couldn't He have heaped blessings on Amy and still called her to pray and write?

As Christians we have to trust God's wisdom in His methods. The overriding sense that all things worked together for good and for God's glory in Amy Carmichael's life, in Job's life, in Abram's, Joseph's, and Paul's lives, helps put our own situations in perspective. The truth Amy Carmichael embraced rings true. God is in control. There are no second causes. When God places us on a path of suffering, we can trust Him to bring good in our lives and glory to His name.

Q: It seems like anger, hate, and unforgiveness are consuming me. I've asked God to take them away. Why hasn't He?

A: Sometimes negative emotions and oppressive thoughts result from physical or mental maladies, which can be treated through counseling or medicine. Depression, fear, anger, and bitterness often devastate or paralyze those who are afflicted by them. During times of suffering, Christians should not be ashamed to pursue professional help.

However, there's more to life than the physical realm. Spiritual enemies seek to destroy us. As long as we remain bitter, Satan knows we will never discern God's goodness in our suffering. As the accuser of the brethren and the father of lies, Satan whispers his poison to the souls of any who will listen. But Satan and his demons have only as much access to our lives as God permits. They, too, are ultimately tools in God's hands.

God allows evil powers to attack His children, because our training as Christians includes spiritual warfare. *Destined for the Throne* (Bethany House, revised 1996), a small, insightful book by Paul E. Billheimer, addresses this topic in detail.

Since we can't *see* the spiritual realm, we are in danger of either trivializing it or becoming obsessed with it. Either way we fall into a ditch. God instructs us to take up the full spiritual armor described in Ephesians 6, but He also reminds us to depend on His protection with the faith of a child. We are victors, because our Father is a mighty warrior. The Word of God is a sword. His written judgments are weapons against Satan. His promises are the downfall of His enemies. When oppressive thoughts overwhelm us, we can declare God's truth to malignant spiritual powers and to our own souls.

As we stand in faith on His truth, He shares His authority over the powers of darkness with us (Eph. 1:18–2:10). Whether the battles are in our external circumstances or in our thoughts, we can overcome through Christ (2 Cor. 10:3–5; Phil. 4:13). God wants us to live peace-filled lives, and He knows we will find true purpose as we overcome Satan and self-centeredness on the battlefield with Him. Every trial is part of our spiritual boot camp, presenting an opportunity for victory and a chance to become more like Christ.

If you've asked God to take away anger, hate, or unforgiveness, but you find yourself still struggling with them, first consider whether the causes may be physical or psychological. You may need professional assistance. However, whether the attacks are primarily physical, psychological, or spiritual, all Christians should study God's Word to learn more about spiritual warfare. It is real, and we are involved in it, whether we acknowledge the fact or not. And we all need to surround ourselves with believers who pray and intercede on our behalf. No one should try to fight the battle alone.

Q: Does God use suffering as punishment for sin?

A: Before we directly address the question, let's lay some groundwork. When we make foolish choices, we suffer consequences. The person who drives drunk and kills a small child will be punished by the law and his own conscience. The child's family will grieve, too. We live in a fallen world, and the actions of those around us affect our lives.

But we are not at the mercy of people's random acts and decisions. God reigns even over choices. This is one of the most perplexing paradoxes in Scripture. Human beings have been given free will. But God's will remains supreme. "The mind of man plans his way, but the LORD directs his steps" (Prov. 16:9).

Romans 9 deals with this difficult topic. In verses 15 and 16, Paul wrote, "For He says to Moses, 'I will have mercy on whom I have mercy, and I will have compassion on whom I have compassion.' So then it does not depend on the man who wills or the man who runs, but on God who has mercy." The chapter goes on to state that God hardened Pharaoh's heart in order to accomplish His will. Does this mean Pharaoh had no choice?

I look at it this way: Yes, people can choose. But an omniscient God knows in advance what each person will choose. If God is powerful enough to speak the universe into existence, He can order events in our lives, shaping our choices. And He has full access to our hearts. We may feel like we're in control, but God is in the driver's seat.

Now, having opened a theological can of worms, let's get back to the original question. Does God use suffering as punishment for sin?

Not all suffering results from sinful choices. Suffering in itself does not indicate God's displeasure. It is not punishment. In fact, Scripture reveals that all who follow Christ will suffer. Jesus Himself—the sinless Son of God—was perfected through suffering (Heb. 5:8–9).

Many Christians live with a burden of false guilt, because we believe the trials and difficulties in our lives reflect God's anger and judgment. We can't manage to get it through our heads that God deliberately puts us in difficult circumstances to help us grow. He loves us too much to leave us in the selfish shallows of life.

When we sin, the Lord convicts us, and there is forgiveness available (1 John 1:9). When tragedy strikes apart from willful sin, we can put our trust in a faithful God:

> Beloved, do not be surprised at the fiery ordeal among you, which comes upon you for your testing, as though some strange thing were happening to you; but to the degree that you share the sufferings of Christ, keep on rejoicing; so that also at the revelation of His glory, you may rejoice with exultation. If you are reviled for the name of Christ, you are blessed, because the Spirit of glory and of God rests on you. Make sure that none of you suffers as a murderer, or thief, or evildoer, or a troublesome meddler; but if anyone suffers as a Christian, he is not to be ashamed, but is to glorify God

in this name. For it is time for judgment to begin with the household of God; and if it begins with us first, what will be the outcome for those who do not obey the gospel of God? And if it is with difficulty that the righteous is saved, what will become of the godless man and the sinner? Therefore, those also who *suffer according to the will of God* shall entrust their souls to a faithful Creator in doing what is right.

(1 Pet. 4:12–19, italics added)

God wills some suffering in our lives because He loves us. Does that mean we should live our lives in dread? Not at all. We should live in joyful gratitude for His amazing blessings, rejoicing in the knowledge that God's mercies are new every morning. We should marvel at the artistry of His creation and let its majesties fill us with awe. Every day holds promise. Every breath is grace.

It is time for judgment to begin with the household of God. We are not a pure and spotless bride yet. But we know our Judge is also our Beloved. May we learn to entrust our souls to Him, knowing He is faithful. And may we open our eyes to see the beauty He is able to create, even out of complete brokenness.